THE STORY OF VICENTE, ‗RED
HIS MOTHER, HIS FATHER, AND SISTER

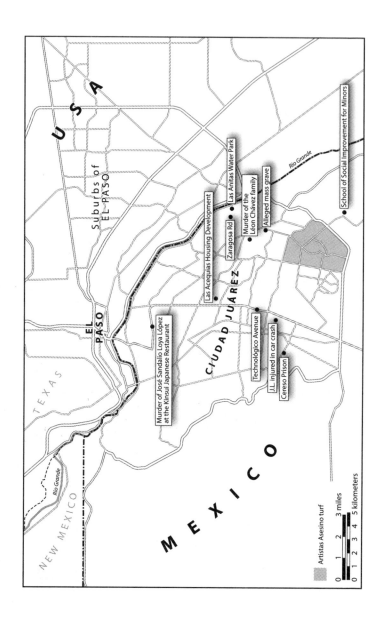

USA

Suburbs of EL PASO

EL PASO

TEXAS

NEW MEXICO

Rio Grande

Rio Grande

MEXICO

CIUDAD JUÁREZ

Las Acequias Housing Development

Zaragosa Rd

Las Anitas Water Park

Murder of the Léon Chávez family

Alleged mass grave

School of Social Improvement for Minors

Murder of José Sandalio Loya López at the Kinsui Japanese Restaurant

Technológico Avenue

J.L. injured in car crash

Cereso Prison

Artistas Asesino turf

0   1   2   3 miles
0 1 2 3 4 5 kilometers

THE STORY OF VICENTE, WHO MURDERED HIS MOTHER, HIS FATHER, AND HIS SISTER

Life and Death in Juárez

SANDRA RODRÍGUEZ NIETO

Translated by
Daniela Maria Ugaz
and
John Washington

VERSO
London • New York

This book has been selected to receive financial assistance from English PEN's Writers in Translation programme supported by Bloomberg. English PEN exists to promote literature and its understanding, uphold writers' freedoms around the world, campaign against the persecution and imprisonment of writers for stating their views, and promote the friendly co-operation of writers and free exchange of ideas.

This paperback edition first published by Verso 2017
First published in English by Verso 2015
Translation © Daniela Maria Ugaz and John Washington 2015, 2017
Originally published as *La fabrica del crimen*
© Temas de Hoy 2012

The moral rights of the author have been asserted

1 3 5 7 9 10 8 6 4 2

Verso
UK: 6 Meard Street, London W1F 0EG
US: 20 Jay Street, Suite 1010, Brooklyn, NY 11201
versobooks.com

Verso is the imprint of New Left Books

ISBN-13: 978-1-78478-105-7
ISBN-13: 978-1-78478-106-4 (US EBK)
ISBN-13: 978-1-78478-107-1 (UK EBK)

British Library Cataloguing in Publication Data
A catalogue record for this book is available from the British Library

The Library of Congress Has Cataloged the Hardback Edition as Follows:
Names: Rodríguez Nieto, Sandra, 1973– author.
Title: The story of Vicente, who murdered his mother, his father, and his
  sister : life and death in Juárez / Sandra Rodríguez Nieto ; translated
  by Daniela Maria Ugaz and John Washington.
Other titles: Fábrica del crimen. English
Description: London ; New York : Verso, 2015. | "Originally published as La
  fabrica del crimen."
Identifiers: LCCN 2015033120 | ISBN 9781784781040 (hbk)
Subjects: LCSH: León Chávez, Vicente, –2009. | León Negrete, Vicente,
  –2004. | Chávez Márquez, Alma Delia, –2004. | Murder—Mexico—Ciudad
  Juâarez—Case studies. | Gangs—Mexico—Ciudad Juárez—Case studies. |
  Youth and violence—Mexico—Ciudad Juárez—Case studies. | Ciudad Juárez
  (Mexico)—Social conditions.
Classification: LCC HV6535.M43 C586513 2015 | DDC 364.152/3092—dc23
LC record available at http://lccn.loc.gov/2015033120

Typeset in Adobe Garamond by MJ&N Gavan, Truro, Cornwall
Printed and bound by CPI Group (UK) Ltd, Croydon, CR0 4YY

For my mom

CONTENTS

I

A CRIME

May 2004: a horn blasts into the night, a car alarm screams. Just south of the US-Mexico border a Ford Explorer without license plates and with its front end wrapped around a tree trunk catches fire. The blaze lights up the darkness of Zaragoza Road, a dirt path cutting through the scattered farm fields of this quadrant of the Río Bravo Valley, the most cultivated area of the otherwise arid outskirts of Ciudad Juárez. Nothing is visible in the darkness except, about 300 yards to the northeast of the smashed Explorer, the water slides of Las Anitas Water Park, silhouetted by the lights of the border wall, which shine down on the dry ditch of desert and split the land in two.

The Explorer wasn't the only car on the road when it caught fire. Nearby was a Jeep Cherokee, which, a few minutes after the Explorer burst into flames, at about three in the morning, took off heading south, away from the border. This isolated strip of Zaragoza Road might seem the perfect place to dump anything that is unwanted. It was really only connected to the urban stain of Juárez by the incongruous waterslide park built in the middle of alternating plots of farm field and wasteland. The night's darkness inundating this stretch of land added to the feeling that distinguishing any person, or any act, would be nearly impossible.

But the nearly abandoned road that the driver of the Cherokee figured to be so perfectly solitary that night was actually the property of businessman Ricardo Escobar, brother of Abelardo Escobar, a member of Mexico's National Action Party (PAN), who two years earlier had been named secretary of agrarian reform under President Felipe Calderón. One of Escobar's night watchmen was the first person interviewed by the state police about what occurred on the night of May 21, 2004. From a small hut built along the edge of a field, the fifty-year-old night watchman was jolted awake by the shrieking car alarm, followed by the growl of the Cherokee speeding away. The racket tore him out of bed, and he ran to his front door, where, facing the international border, he could see a burst of flame and, close to one of the poplar trees that hugged the border wall, what he thought was a second truck whose color and model were too dark for him to distinguish. He left the hut to see what was going on but then heard a series of explosions. He would later tell the investigators that he wanted to call the police, but he didn't have a phone. Meanwhile, the Cherokee made a slow getaway, bouncing over the potholes and rubble of the dirt road.

The burning car was reported to the fire department an hour and a half later when, from his patrol car on the Zaragoza International Bridge, a police officer saw what looked to be a brushfire along the edge of the river.

Four months previously, a group of state policemen had been identified as the perpetrators of the kidnapping and murder of twelve persons whose bodies were discovered in the very heart of central Juárez, in an outdoor patio of the housing development Las Acequias. The policemen were accused of working for the Carrillo Fuentes Cartel (also known as the Juárez Cartel), which controlled all the drug-trafficking points in the state of Chihuahua at the time, including the five border crossings between Juárez and the United States. But even after the prosecution and disbandment of the criminally involved policemen, murders and gunfights continued to plague the city. That same year, there were a total of twenty-three victims executed cartel-style; in the previous week alone, there had been four. Though the policeman on Zaragoza International Bridge thought it was only a brushfire, the current spate of violence spurred him to take a closer look.

Firemen came. They fought the blaze for over an hour, the sinister yellow flames flickering along with the flashing blue and red emergency lights.

"Let's get out of here," one cop said to the first responding officer.

"Nope. You guys stay. This truck may just have a gift for us."

It was after five in the morning, the sky already beginning to blush, when the cops could finally see through the smoke to the blackened skeleton of the truck with the soft-top back. A fireman was the first to approach and peer inside. What he found, he would later say in an interview, was more shocking than anything he had seen in a six-year career fighting fires: the burnt remains of three bodies, almost completely ravaged by the flames, lying on the collapsed backseat. Each of the body's skulls had exploded in the heat of the fire. One of the bodies didn't have arms or legs anymore. He could see a spine through an open chest cavity. One of the bodies, he noticed, was significantly smaller than the other two.

This was the "gift" the officers had waited for.

Some six hours earlier, on the evening of Thursday, May 20, three teenagers drove around in an old cherry-red Dodge Intrepid a few miles south of Zaragoza Road on the unpaved Rosita Road, cutting across vacant lots and a smattering of residential areas, farms and garbage dumps. This was the boundary line between the shores of the Rio Grande and the fanning edge of the Chihuahua Desert.

Bouncing over potholes in the Intrepid was a scrawny, brown-skinned teenager and his two best friends. The scrawny kid in the passenger seat was sixteen-year-old Vicente León Chávez, student of the Colegio de Bachilleres 6, the only high school in the Juárez Valley. Driving the car was Eduardo, a seventeen-year-old El Paso native, who had become Vicente's inseparable friend after the two met at the beginning of the fourth quarter of school that same year. Uziel Guerrero, who Vicente had known for years, dozed in the backseat; he was eighteen years old.

Hidden under his white collared school uniform shirt, Vicente had a .38 caliber pistol tucked between his belt and his gray slacks. On their way to his house, Vicente spoke to Eduardo in a clipped, demanding tone.

"It has to be today. Tomorrow is Friday. And then the banks close on Saturdays."

"Well, then let's do it next week," reasoned Eduardo. "I mean, we've already got the gun."

"No way," Vicente insisted, his quick temper already swelling. "I only get to keep it for a day."

Vicente was used to giving orders. He spoke to his friends firmly, often raising his voice to force his ideas on them. He thought he was smarter than them, and often told them so. For years he'd ordered Uziel to keep his mouth shut because "he was an idiot," and because only one of them could ever be right. Without quite knowing why, Uziel had tolerated this ever since they'd studied together at the Secundaria Técnica 44, their middle school, where they'd already shared their bad grades and worse reputations. In the short time since they'd met, Eduardo had also found Vicente to be an indispensable friend, and he forgave him anything. Though Eduardo had a subdued demeanor, and differentiated himself from the other two by his good performance in school, his grade point average had started to dip since getting to know Vicente, who was a drinker, dabbled in pot, ecstasy and mushrooms, and had a reckless and devil-may-care attitude. Of course, that was what Eduardo and Uziel found so enticing about him.

The adrenaline of their friendship had risen to a feverish pitch since Vicente and Eduardo had begun scheming on how to get a gun, especially after Vicente had told Eduardo what he planned to do with it. For hours they'd amble the streets of Melchor Ocampo, considered one of Juárez's most dangerous neighborhoods, openly asking every *cholo* they bumped into where they could buy or rent a piece.

Uziel was largely unaware of his friends' conspiracy until that Thursday, the night he planned to take a girl out to a billiards hall in the suburb where he lived. Uziel had long ago abandoned his parents' evangelism, which he may have once used to reason himself out of potential trouble, and he was now so far removed from any moral grounding that when his best friend told him what he wanted to do that night, he was taken aback, but only for a moment, and quickly responded that he'd help him on the condition that they do it early enough so that he wouldn't miss his date.

He would miss it. It was already eleven at night when he awoke in the backseat of the car as Eduardo parked in front of Vicente's house. The cool spring wind whipped them in the face as they stepped into the night and began strolling the bald, sidewalkless streets. The streetlights cast a dim amber spotlight on a row of gray houses surrounded by a dark smudge of land, bare except for a few trees and Vicente's father's zinc-roofed auto-repair shop.

A small address plaque can still be seen on the corner of Vicente's house. It says: "5824 Rosita Road. God Bless Our Home."

Vicente paused on the front porch before stepping inside his house.

"Maybe we shouldn't yet," he said. "We need more bullets. I only have one."

"Fine with me," Eduardo responded.

The three stood in silence. Vicente, taller than the other two, observed his friends from above. It wasn't true about the single bullet. He only wanted to gain time and find a way to convince one of them to pull the trigger for him. He wondered if he would actually be able to talk them into it.

Uziel was getting nervous. His survival instinct, run-down as it was, told him that this time Vicente had gone too far, that he was serious about wanting to use the pistol. Uziel had known Vicente for years; he knew what he was capable of.

"We're gonna flip for it, see who pulls the trigger," Vicente said. The other two boys looked at him, surprised and nervous. Was he serious?

"Remember about that two hundred thousand dollar ransom," he insisted. "I already told you, everyone's gonna think it was a narco job."

In the strained silence, Vicente took three coins out of his pocket, giving one to Uziel and one to Eduardo. He flicked his own coin into the air, catching it and slapping it on his wrist. As usual, Eduardo and Uziel imitated him without a second thought. A moment later, Uziel had lost.

"No," Uziel said. "I can't do it." Just this once, he wanted to stand up to Vicente.

"Don't be an idiot," Vicente replied. "You already said you would."

Something in Vicente's voice and mannerisms always seemed irrefutable to Uziel, as if a law had been laid down, one of the very few that proved unbreakable to him. So used to obeying his friend, he hardly noticed that he had already taken the gun into his hand.

"Alright! You got the gun now," Vicente said. "It's on you. Let's roll."

Uziel tried to give the pistol back, explaining with as much conviction as he could muster, "I'm not doing a thing. They're your parents, and they're your problem. You shoot."

Vicente stopped trying to convince him and took the gun. He knew that soon enough he'd make his friend fulfill the destiny of the coin toss. Momentum was the only thing that mattered now, getting into the house and finishing off what he'd decided to do.

*   *   *

Vicente was sick of his family.

He couldn't stand his father, who seemed to enjoy punishing him, yelling and cursing at him for sport. He hated his mother too, who never came to his defense and always pointed out his mistakes. But who he especially detested, more than anybody else, was his little sister, Laura Ivette, a sweet thirteen-year-old girl who, like her brother, had a clear complexion, big, slightly drooping eyes, a fine nose and thick eyebrows. Calm, studious and obedient, Laura Ivette was adored by her friends at school. It seemed everyone who knew her loved her. Plus, or so Vicente believed, she was obviously their parents' favorite. But to Vicente, more than anything, she was a hypocrite. Behind everyone's back, she would sneak up to him and antagonize him, rubbing it in that her parents had already bought her a car so she could start driving to school. And they were never going to give *him* a car, Laura Ivette would hiss. And not having a car meant that he'd have to keep riding an hour each way on the crammed, bouncing micro-buses, those old clunkers that wound their way around the city for an hour before dropping him off at school. In the summer afternoons, the lack of AC in the battered buses left him bathed in sweat before class. He would counter the heat and boredom by drinking nearly a whole liter of beer on the bus, making him famous among his school friends for being a drunk. His teachers, meanwhile, considered him nothing more than a pest.

But aside from Uziel and Eduardo, nobody would have imagined that the only thing on Vicente's mind those days was wiping out his family, killing them all except for little C.E., his three-year-old brother and the only person in the world for whom he felt true affection.

"We've given it enough thought," Vicente said, walking into the house.

A living room and kitchen fanned out behind the blanched wood of the front door. Vicente flicked on the light.

The family home was bigger than average for this part of Juárez. The living room alone spanned 215 square feet. On the left, there was a hallway leading to the master bedroom, where the parents, Vicente León Negrete and Alma Delia Chávez Márquez, forty and thirty-six years old, respectively, were watching television with the window open, enjoying the night's soft breeze, completely unaware of what was going on in their son's head.

Laura Ivette, dreaming of her crushes, slept in her own bedroom on the other side of the hallway. C.E. had fallen asleep at her side.

"Let's go to my room," Vicente said, snapping off the light and leaving the living room in shadow, as it would remain the rest of the night. The three boys shuffled into Vicente's bedroom, which abutted the living room. Uziel and Eduardo sat on a twin bed framed by a brown and yellow headboard, Vicente on a plastic chair facing the bed.

The three of them, still wearing their school uniforms, took turns with the gun, passing it around, cocking it, aiming it, posing as gang bangers. Soon, however, they seemed to forget about the murder and started talking about the school field trip they'd have the next day: in celebration of National Student Day they were going to Las Anitas Water Park.

But Vicente's thoughts didn't waver for long, and he tiptoed out of the room a few times to sneak a peek at his parents. The last time he checked on them he returned with a kitchen knife, handing it to Eduardo.

"Just in case," he said. "You follow Uziel, and if he doesn't pull it off, you'll know what to do."

Vicente had the attitude down: his voice aggressive and commanding, his gait confident, even insolent, like someone about to commit a crime. He convinced his friends that they only needed to wait until his parents were asleep, and then they would kill them with ease. More importantly, they should be thinking of what they were going to do with the money they'd soon have. Nobody, he assured them, *ever*, without a doubt, would find out what had happened.

A little after midnight, Vicente got up one last time to check on his parents. When he returned to his room he took up the pistol and gave it to Uziel.

"They're sleeping now," he said. "Come on, ándale. It's time."

"No," Uziel responded.

"¡Ándale! You lost the coin toss, remember." Vicente was using that manipulative tone he knew worked so well on Uziel. "¡Ándale!" he said again.

Uziel took the gun and walked out of the room, but then almost immediately tried to get back in.

"No," he said, softly. "I'm not going to do it."

"What do you mean you're not going to do it? Think about how much money we could make. ¡Ándale!" Vicente's tone sharpened, rising above the insistent whisper he'd been using.

"Vicente," a voice called. "Is that you?"

It was Alma Delia, his mother, calling to him from bed.

"¡Ándale!" Vicente said again, getting behind Uziel and pushing him toward the master bedroom. "Just imagine," he whispered into his friend's ear, "riding in a brand new car."

Uziel walked down the dark hallway, the pistol clutched in his right hand. He stopped in front of the bedroom door.

"Do it!" Vicente ordered, opening the bedroom door.

Uziel closed his eyes, slightly turned his head away, and fired twice. One of the bullets hit Vicente León Negrete in the chest, piercing his lung.

In the room, lit by the flickering television, Alma Delia could just make out the blood starting to flow from her husband's wound and his open, already dead eyes.

Uziel ran off, down the hallway and onto the front porch. Vicente darted into the bathroom and closed the door behind him.

Left alone in the hallway, Eduardo walked to the bedroom door to see what his friends had done. Blood was pouring out of Vicente's father. Stunned, Eduardo hardly noticed the screams of Alma Delia, who was still lying next to her dead husband. The weight she had gained over the years labored her movements, her shock and fear seeming to anchor her in place.

Still in the doorway, Eduardo felt a presence behind him.

"The knife," Vicente said. "It's your turn." He gave him a little nudge, speaking in the same tone he had used with Uziel, the same tone Vicente's father used with him.

"It's El Güero!" Alma Delia screamed, using Eduardo's nickname.

"Do it!" Vicente ordered.

"Vicente," his mother screamed. "Help! Why are you shooting at us?"

"It wasn't me," he said to his mother, then whispered to Eduardo, "Kill her."

The wailing, the blood and the confusion all stirring together, Eduardo nearly dove into the room, knife-first.

"But Lalo!" Alma Delia screamed. "Why?" She stretched

her arms out, groping the air, trying in vain to defend herself from the attack.

"I wish I knew, ma'am," Eduardo responded. "Ask your son!"

She screamed.

Eduardo was only able to quiet her with the knife. The glowing TV silhouetted his body and cloaked Alma Delia in shadow, hiding her face of pain and panic. He could hear nothing but wheezing as he stabbed her two, three, four, twelve more times. He punctured her neck, her thorax, her abdomen, and then he smelled the nauseating whiff of blood. Had it not been for the sudden pain that shot through his head and slid to the bottom of his stomach, Eduardo would have continued, almost unconsciously, destroying the body of his friend's mother. When he regained some sense of consciousness, he wasn't even able to take a moment to see what he had done because he had to race to the bathroom, fighting to contain his vomit before reaching the toilet.

A girl's voice called from the hallway. It was Laura Ivette. Still half asleep, she crept out of her room. Her hair was down and disheveled, her white pajamas and her half-shut eyes accentuating the innocence of the question she had for her brother.

"What's going on?"

"Nothing," Vicente responded, hooking his arm around her neck and stabbing her with a kitchen knife, sinking it into her nine times. The teenager's body, so fragile, took only a few minutes to succumb to the loss of blood from her shredded vital organs.

Eduardo, on his way out of the bathroom, could see into the dark hallway as Vicente strangled and stabbed his sister.

Instinctively, he made his way to the front door, which Uziel had left open when he had wildly fled to the porch. He closed the door behind him and saw Uziel, who was trembling, covering his ears, slapping his forehead, and still clutching the gun.

"Get inside," Eduardo demanded. "You can't be outside with the gun. The cops might drive by."

When they turned back to the living room, they saw Laura Ivette's body on the floor. She was motionless, face down, a pillowcase already over her head. Vicente ordered them to the bedroom: they needed covers and sheets for the bodies. He went to get the Explorer that one of his father's clients had left behind. He reversed it until it nuzzled against the patio door and then reached back and reclined the backseats before getting out and opening the hatch. Eduardo came out onto the patio and cut a piece of blue tarpaulin that had been covering one of the cars. He used it to wrap up Laura Ivette's small corpse and then, with Uziel's help, he lugged the body to the door. They heaved it through the trunk of the Explorer, where it slumped into the backseat.

In the bedroom, Uziel looked at the other two bodies. That they would somehow, somewhere, dump them had been the only step in this crime that they'd easily agreed upon. After killing the parents, they figured, it would be simple enough to get the bodies in a car and look for a place to dispose of them. If Uziel and Eduardo believed in one thing that Vicente had told them, it was that this part would be a breeze, that no one would ever find out who had killed them.

"Make peace with your mother," Uziel said to Vicente.

By the bedside, Vicente hoisted his mother by an arm, Eduardo taking the other arm, Uziel the feet. They set her on top of a blanket, dragged her from the bedroom to the patio, and hoisted her up again in order to slump her over the rear passenger-side seat.

Then they came back for Vicente's father, who they also wrapped in a sheet. But when they tried to move his body, they saw that his blood had coagulated all over his back, and it was so thick that it had stuck to the mattress. Vicente rushed to the kitchen and came back with a pitcher of water to try to wash it off. He then lifted his father's body by an arm, Uziel took the other arm, and Eduardo, this time, the feet. Again they crossed the house, made it to the patio and heaved the man's body into the backseat, next to the body of Laura Ivette, who slumped sideways until she rested on her father.

Only then did Vicente turn on the lights in the house. All along the hallway, red stains formed a trail between the bedroom and the door. He took the pitcher, filled it with water again and emptied it on the floor. He stripped the beds and pillows of their sheets and pillowcases, picked up the knife, which had ended up on a dresser, and dumped it all on top of the bodies in the van. From the patio he got a bucket and mop. Uziel and Eduardo, meanwhile, sat on a living-room sofa, observing Vicente's frenetic cleaning, who at some point had taken off his gray school uniform pants, which the other two still wore.

"What are we going to do with the bodies?" Uziel asked.

"We'll have to burn them," Vicente answered. "Any idea where we could ditch them? Somewhere over by your house maybe?"

"There's an empty lot past Fidel Ávila."

"Fine. I'll take the Explorer and you guys can follow me in one of the shop cars. Take my dad's Cherokee. The keys are inside."

Vicente walked out to the patio and went to the small storage shed on a corner of the lot, where his dad kept his work tools. He took the keys to the Explorer, a gallon of gasoline and a bottle of Reduce, a flammable solvent used to strip paint off car parts. He opened the front gate, got behind the wheel and set off. Eduardo and Uziel got into the Cherokee and followed him, heading north down dusty Rosita Road. A little up the way, Vicente came to a stop and waited for his friends to pull up next to him.

"Where to?" Vicente asked.

"Where we said," Uziel answered. "Just drive." And he sped off, letting Vicente trail behind him.

From Rosita Road, in their pair of unregistered cars, past the bars, cheap restaurants and motels that cluster near and around Zaragoza Bridge, the boys took Ejercito Nacional Avenue, which crosses Juárez-Porvenir Street and, a little farther down, turns into Internacional Avenue, or, as it's known in English, Waterfill Road. They turned north on Nardos Street, a wide, unpaved artery on which expansive McMansions adorned with balustrades are interspersed with abandoned housing developments and vacant lots. Passing one such lot, cattycorner to a playground, the Cherokee took a right, toward the Rio Grande, driving about 100 yards through fields of crops on a chalky path encircled by trees. This was Zaragoza Road.

"Stop." Uziel's command seemed to fall from the encompassing darkness. They had only the lights of the border wall to illuminate a distant point in their path. "We've got to wait for Vicente." When Vicente arrived and pulled up on their passenger side, Uziel told him to drive ahead, as deep into the brush as he could.

Vicente obeyed, driving a few yards until he came to a tree where he braked, briefly, before slamming on the accelerator and crashing the Explorer. He exited the car, took the gallon of gas and the flammable solvent and, along with Uziel, started to douse the inside of the van, the seats, the dashboard, the floor, the bodies of his mother, his father, his little sister.

"Get out of the way," Uziel ordered him before fishing a lighter out of his pocket, setting the car ablaze and sprinting away.

Eduardo waited for them with the Cherokee running and, when Uziel and Vicente got in, sped off in the opposite direction of the river. It was around three in the morning.

"Go to my house," Vicente said as they passed through the city. The boys were so convinced of having committed the perfect crime that they even dared to drive a few miles out of the way on Internacional Avenue to buy hydrochloric acid at a twenty-four-hour Bip Bip convenience store. The employee attending them failed to notice the bloodstains through the drive-through window.

When they got back to the house, Vicente used the acid to wipe down everything in sight, from the floor to the door handles, the dressers, the fans, especially the beds. With Eduardo's help, Vicente turned over the mattresses and made the beds with clean sheets. His friends were tired now and wanted to go home. In silence, they peeled off their gray school uniform pants and put on some of Vicente's clothes.

Vicente slinked into the room where his little brother, C.E., was still sleeping and sat down next to him.

"What are you going to do about your little brother?" Uziel asked from the doorway.

"He'll be OK. I'll get him out of Juárez and take him to a ranch."

"Take the Cherokee," Vicente said to them. "Remember, you've got to come back in the morning. Then we'll decide what to do."

When Uziel and Eduardo left, it was almost five in the morning. At that hour the yolk of sun was just breaking in the morning sky, and from every direction buses taking commuters to their factory jobs were rumbling through the streets.

Alone in his house, Vicente continued to wash away the blood. Bloody shoe prints were everywhere, in the kitchen, in the hallway—he had to go out to the patio spigot several times to refill his bucket with clean water. Along with the stains, he washed away all of his parents' unjustified reprimands, the promises they took back without explanation, the constant pressure to obey rules he didn't understand, the feeling of having to belong to a group of people with which he couldn't communicate. Then he washed away the stain of humiliation that was Laura Ivette, their parents' favorite, for whom they had even bought a car.

Vicente finished cleaning around six in the morning. He crept back into C.E.'s room and covered him in a blanket, wrapped him in his arms and brought him to his parents' bedroom. There on his parents' bed he cuddled with his baby brother and fell asleep until ten in the morning on Friday, May 21, 2004.

2

THE CITY

It was a Saturday evening, October 25, 1997, in the neighborhood of La Rosita, only a few hundred feet from Vicente's house.

A nine-foot-high white gate towered over 747 Luna Street with a crown of spiraling barbed wire. Without objection, the guard opened the door as soon as he heard the order bellowed from the street below, where close to fifty federal and state police officers had gathered. They had arrived en masse to inspect the house on the corner of Jilatopec Street and Juárez-Porvenir Highway, which connects Juárez Valley to the Zaragoza International Bridge. On the grounds, the police found a car lot that supposedly had been used by various members of the Juárez Cartel. The state prosecutor's office informed the press that they'd found twenty-one cars, many of them luxury models. Neatly aligned, as if on display on the 3,000-square-foot cement patio, was a white armored dump truck, a black Ram Charger with Mexico City plates, armored as well as outfitted with gold encrusted mirrors and trimmings, a navy blue Suburban, a Ford Mustang and a yellow Corvette, among many others. The lot stretched to the south, spilling out to a gazebo fashioned with outdoor grills and framed by more layers of fence, fledgling palm trees and twenty-foot-tall outdoor lamps, which, still today, are clearly visible from miles away.

The neighbors who were questioned claimed to have seen luxury sports cars and trucks and heavily armed men continuously flitting in and out of the house.

Vicente León would turn ten years old two days later, on Monday, October 27. But even before the raid of the lot, the neighborhood of La Rosita was rife with criminal activity. Years earlier, the body of a man stabbed to death had been dumped in the neighborhood's dry irrigation canal. Shortly after, another body had been found in the charred skeleton of a burned car trunk.

Violence was on the rise not only in La Rosita but all over the city, especially since 1993, when the annual number of homicides rose from fifty-five to more than 120 in just one year, a figure that would be outdone every following year to the present day.* In 1997, there were close to 250 murders across the city, most occurring after the death of Amado Carrillo Fuentes, who had become the top hand of the Juárez Cartel in 1993, when the previous kingpin, the ex–federal police officer Rafael Aguilar, was killed.

Until 1997, however, for many people in Juárez, the violence was observed as though from afar. The city was enjoying a stunning financial boom as well as surging population growth. In the last decade of the twentieth century, Juárez

---

* The original version of *The Story of Vicente* was published in 2012; since then it is cautiously believed that the homicide rate has dropped.

went from being a medium-sized city to the capital of Mexico's manufacturing industry. Dozens of transnational corporations subcontracted companies to send recruiting buses to southern Mexico, reeling in tens of thousands of people who, at a rate of almost 100,000 per year, joined the industrious, boisterous life of the border city. The population rose at a rate never before recorded in any part of Mexico when Juárez became a paradise of employment in the same decade in which, with the passing of the North Atlantic Free Trade Agreement in 1994, the country at large lost thousands of jobs in agriculture, an industry that was dealt a nearly mortal blow by US agribusiness. It was then that for millions of people throughout Mexico the maquiladora and the drug cartels became the only sources of employment. Juárez was the mecca of both industries. Though the drug business was hardly mentioned, all across Mexico the maquiladora was seen as the "great motor" that would keep money flowing at a constantly rising rate. Maquiladoras—which at the time primarily manufactured auto parts, from screws to seat-belt buckles—employed laborers who required transportation, housing and dozens of goods and services, from food, schools and shoes to entertainment and communication, steadily driving up development until there wasn't a commercial pocket empty of newly booming opportunity. Money flowed, as did the seemingly ceaseless construction of industrial warehouses and shopping malls and, especially in the southeast, the development of thousands of units of low-income housing for factory laborers. There were also thousands of new and used cars circulating the streets, thanks to American car owners who traded older vehicles for the newest models by the millions each year. Like never before, people in Juárez went out in the evenings for food and flashy entertainment to the dozens of overflowing bars and restaurants. They were accompanied by a steady stream of American tourists, still coming to enjoy the bustle and cheap goods south of the border.

But even then Juárez showed telltale signs that the money generated by maquiladoras and drug trafficking, the two pillars of industrial and commercial euphoria, was failing to trickle down to the masses or translate into better quality of life for newly arrived Juárenses. For years, almost half a million people lived in hamlets on the foothills of the western Sierra, nestled between ravines, the roads unpaved and without any basic services. In the southeast, another wave of inhabitants was forced to live even farther from the city hub, separated by thousands of acres left abandoned in the midst of the building boom, populated only by sand and trash. Like islands in a sea of wasteland and grit, even the wealthy neighborhoods were forced to settle on the far side of these badlands. In the evenings and early mornings, with everyone rushing to or from work, these tracts of empty land proved nearly impossible to navigate.

If the stained cityscape was ominous, there were other and more disturbing signs begging us to question the supposed benefits of the rise of maquila employment. Living in the city was like playing Russian roulette. Violence and death tore through our neighborhoods with a surging intensity, as if to prove that the spiking social and political inequalities—the $60-a-week poverty wages parceled out by transnational companies, the glaring corruption of local politicians and the generalized marginalization of Juárez's citizens—would be paid for in human lives. Between 1993 and 1997, at least 150 women had been murdered, their bodies found littered across the city. By the late 1990s, the recently termed crime of "femicide" had been widely reported on by local media, hooking the attention of feminist circles, and, in 1997, finally becoming part of the national discourse. The brutality of the murders and the haphazard way in which the women's bodies were dumped in the dirt like trash was evidence that even then there was widespread contempt for human life, the implications and lessons of which we still cannot seem to grasp. Just as we weren't able to understand the effects of another extremely violent phenomenon, also on the rise in 1997: the kidnappings of men, which struck hundreds of families—many of them middle class—who one day came home to find their doors broken down, their houses ravaged, their clothes scattered on the floor, and the sudden absence of their son, father, husband or brother, who they would never again see. These abductions were characterized by their lack of public attention and by the fact that they were used, in the logic of narco trafficking, to even the score among rival cartels. There were hundreds of kidnapping victims on both sides of the border, as well as more than 1,000 men found murdered in the city since 1993.

By 1997, Amado Carrillo had made us all well aware that since he'd taken the reins four years previously the Juárez Cartel had worked its way to becoming one of the most influential organized crime groups in Mexico. Carrillo had an air fleet that shuttled vast amounts of drugs from Colombia, a show of power that earned him the title "the Lord of the Skies." For years the cartel had enjoyed the protection of the military, the police and various political sectors, giving the Lord of the Skies near total immunity. Pushing drugs across the border was a multimillion-dollar business, and in Juárez we had come to accept that some of the profits were used to finance other businesses, including, to name just a few, restaurants, hotels, bars, event halls, hospitals, real estate companies, gyms and agribusinesses.

But even as the human suffering became more evident, soaring profits throughout the city overshadowed the violence. It seemed only the families of the victims were the ones mourning or paying any attention to the murders, and because of the utter inefficacy of the Mexican justice system, Juárenses were left in the dark about the motives or the details of the crimes, forcing many to come up with their own insufficient explanations, which, over the years, gave way to a sort of collective blindness. We were unable to truly see the victims. Unable to see our own indignation and fear, and without an official explanation to guide us, we developed our own theories to explain away the violence. The abducted men, for example, were immediately deemed narco criminals and dumped into the mass grave of suspicion, the blanket lie of "*en algo andarán*," or "they were *involved*." The femicides, however, were much harder to resolve in our collective imagination, which is why theories surrounding them multiplied. Though I had little idea who was responsible, one thing was clear to me, and that was that the city's physical makeup was itself conducive to crime. It was enough to see the expanding empty plots of land to imagine suffering an attack without anyone being around to help you, let alone hear your screams. Many of the bodies of the murdered women were left discarded in the Lote Bravo, an enormous plateau of dirt that stretches from the Rio Grande to the southeastern dunes, where Juárez was just starting to build new shack·communities. The Juárez landscape was especially threatening at night, and so we came to understand that women died for being poor and for having to trek such inhospitable routes to work and back. Men died for being narcos, women for being alone. That is how we explained away the fear, the imminent danger we all lived in.

Like Janus, the two-faced Greek god of choices and cross-roads, Juárez had another side to it that was totally apart from the violence reported in the news. In fact, life in Juárez could be full of happiness and success, despite it being a physically amorphous hub, both dirty and ugly. In the '90s, the city was a place that gave hundreds of thousands of people a feeling of security and prosperity that can only come from knowing that you have a job and a reliable means of income. The lavish employment opportunities were seen as solutions to all of life's ills. Wages were euphorically reinvested in the consumption of alcohol, a passion that seemed to be shared by a large percentage of the population, both men and women. The love of the ubiquitous nightlife entertainment even gave the city a democratic air: there seemed to be a place for everyone. Nothing would be able to stop the economic frenzy. Yes, there were murders and forced disappearances, but the shadows that guarded the inner workings of crime from our eyes gave us the perception that the murders happened somewhere else, committed by the hands of who knows who, with who knows what motives. So why should we be scared? And who should we be scared of?

But then, in the second half of 1997, there was a sudden and significant change in the patterns of violence. In July, after Amado Carrillo's unexpected death during a plastic surgery operation in Mexico City, the citizens of Juárez witnessed a rise in the homicide rate that, for the first time, showcased the murderous muscle behind the Juárez Cartel. The organization that until then had followed the standard pattern of violence, using the more cosmetic "silent disappearances," now started evening the score with blood-spattering displays of vengeance. The first hit occurred on the night of Sunday, August 3, at a restaurant called Max Fim, where a group of men armed with AK-47s shot to death Alfonso Corral Olague, a thirty-six-year-old man from Durango and an alleged collaborator of the Juárez Cartel. Five others died in the shootout: one of Corral's girlfriends, one of his guards and three innocent bystanders, including a couple eating at an adjacent table. It was clear that new rules had been set. The government's number one rule—keeping violence out of the public eye—was no longer going to be followed. Two weeks later, there was another public shootout, this time in plain daylight, targeting the lawyer Ricardo Prado Reynal, who allegedly helped found various money laundering businesses. The next day, four doctors who worked at a hospital owned by the families targeted at Max Fim were found strangled to death, left piled one on top of the other on a dirt road a few yards from the Rio Grande. A week later, the Juárez Cartel killed three more people as they left a bar called Gerónimo's, next door to Max Fim. Among the victims was José Guzman, businessman and brother of the 1995 Miss Mexico.

Most of these murders occurred on the same street, Paseo Triunfo de la República (Triumph of the Republic Avenue), near a defunct bullfighting plaza. And, according to the deputy attorney general of the National Action Party, the murders were connected and "undoubtedly" orchestrated by organized crime groups.

The investigation at the property on Luna Street in the La

Rosita neighborhood soon set off another violent settling of accounts, what was becoming a common occurrence in the latter half of 1997. José Sandalio Loya López, a thirty-two-year-old businessman and owner of the auto plating company that bulletproofed the luxury cars found on the premises, seemed to have crossed a line in explaining to authorities that, because of its convenient proximity to the Zaragoza International Bridge, the estate served well as a logistical center and warehouse for the Juárez Cartel. The tip-off cost him his life. On November 15, two weeks after the police investigation in La Rosita, while Loya was eating at the Japanese restaurant Kinsui, also on Paseo Triunfo de la República, a man dressed in black walked in and shot Loya three times, once in the neck and twice in the head. That very gun, it was later discovered, was used in the murder of the lawyer Prado Reynal, seeming to confirm that the same assassin was employed for both murders. Although Loya had a .40 caliber pistol tucked in his belt, he never had a chance to draw it. He bled to death in his chair, still waiting for his sushi.

That September, two months before his death, Loya had registered a new company, Blindajes Nacionales de Mexico (National Vehicle Fortification of Mexico), which, according to information revealed in the search, was employed to bulletproof the cars of the Juárez Cartel. Officially, however, Loya had a stake as an adviser to Miguel Lucer Palma, a federal representative of the Institutional Revolutionary Party, who had made sure to supply him with the official credential that was used to identify him at the scene of his death.

Arturo Chávez Chávez, the PAN deputy attorney general for Francisco Barrio—who a year later became the national attorney general under President Felipe Calderón—characterized the series of shootings and murders of the latter half of 1997 as the settling of "outstanding debts" between competing inheritors of the dead drug lord Amado Carrillo. One such inheritor—eager to shed blood until he rose to the top—was the brother of Amado, Vicente Carrillo.

And yet, well after Amado's death, the rush of publicly displayed violence continued, spreading through the city, bodies being dumped everywhere. It hit La Rosita neighborhood first. In 1998, local media reported that two bodies were found in the trunk of a car left on Rosita Road, close to Vicente León's house. Both of the deceased were male, naked, gagged and showed signs of strangulation. In 2001, another body was found in La Rosita. The victim, the thirty-second homicide of the year, dead from a bullet to the head, was found with his hands and feet tied with metal wire. La Rosita, like much of Juárez, seemed to be perfect for this type of crime: long uninhabited tracts of wasteland that were swallowed by complete darkness at night. The wide arroyo that cut through La Rosita was so deserted that people were afraid to walk through it even during the day.

The property on Luna Street, referred to by the media as "the bunker," provoked continued suspicion. Soon after the 1997 report of the luxury narco vehicles, there were rumors that the property could also have served as a common graveyard for *levantones* (literally, those who are lifted, usually victims of cartel kidnapping). Further fuel was added to the rumor in 1999 when Mexican officials, along with US FBI agents, reported the discovery of six bodies secretly buried in a ranch called La Campana, located along the Juárez Highway en route to the neighborhood of Casas Grandes.

The owner of the La Campana property, Jesús Ortiz

Gutiérrez, also owned the bunker in La Rosita. In 1999, the attorney general's Special Organized Crimes Unit (UEDO in Spanish) detained Gutiérrez and shuttled him to Mexico City. The government later seized his property. Ortiz's lawyer, Ignacio Esqueda, maintained that he was innocent of any wrongdoing and expressed outrage that both his client and the security guard of the property were being held in solitary confinement. With Esqueda's help, Ortiz was eventually able to regain legal control of the properties by 2000. Meanwhile, for years, the rumor that the bunker had buried human remains continued to circulate among victims' grieving family members. In November of 2003, on the fourth anniversary of the disinterment of the bodies, various family members of the disappeared held a rally demanding that in the same way the La Campana Ranch was searched, the concrete patio of the bunker should be dug up and properly investigated. The protestors told reporters that they had formally asked the attorney general to launch another investigation because of the persistent rumors that the patio had served as an arena for executions, torture and secret burials. The hope, said protestor Lorenza Benavides, was that they would find the rest of the victims who had been "disappeared" by the cartels, a figure that by 2003 had climbed to 700 people. They feared that the concrete parking lot was built for the sole reason of hiding a burial ground.

The family members continued the search for their loved ones openly and tirelessly, seemingly indifferent to the growing stigmatization of their grief. El Paso native Patricia Garibay explained to reporter Rosa Isela Pérez: "I never denied that my brother was a drug trafficker, but nobody has the right to disappear anybody else. We want him back." For five years

Garibay had been searching incessantly for her brother, Jorge, whose disappearance was one of the most widely publicized cases in Juárez.

Jorge was thirty years old when he decided, one night in January 1998, to celebrate a successful cocaine delivery to El Paso with two of his accomplices. The three men were in Club Kentucky, one of the oldest bars on Juárez Avenue and only two blocks from the Santa Fe International Bridge, when a group of armed men busted into the bar and dragged Garibay out, racing away without leaving a trace. As Garibay was also a US citizen, the FBI began an investigation that finally led to the excavation of the La Campana Ranch. Garibay's body, however, was not among those found at the ranch. An informant described harrowing scenes of hundreds of people kidnapped by the cartel to be tortured (so that they would "sing" important information), then executed and buried on small farms and ranches throughout Juárez, many of which were not discovered until years later. Patricia Garibay described living in constant torture herself: that there wasn't a day that would pass without the family asking themselves what could have happened to Jorge, or where his body could be. Sometimes she felt resigned, Patricia described, while other times she would feel angry and thirst for revenge. "And then again we'd feel resigned and suffer that constant will to find him," she said at the 2003 rally outside of the property on Luna Street. She explained that losing a loved one and not knowing if he is dead or alive is worse than simply knowing he's dead. Families remain in an unending state of anguish, haunted by the idea that at any moment their child or brother could be tortured, or could be buried alone somewhere, in total aban-donment. It's why, she said, she and her family will never give up. Since the initial disinterment in 1999, members of the Association of Families and Friends of Disappeared Persons in Juárez have continued to rally outside of properties they suspect could contain common graves.

"The bunker" of La Rosita was searched for the last time in February 2004, an important moment in Juárez's recent history. On January 23 of the same year, the attorney general's office, in collaboration with the US government, found a corpse buried in the front yard of a house in the neighborhood of Las Acequias, just off of Tecnológico Avenue. The house number was 3633 Parsioneros Street. A few days later, officials found another eleven bodies. The discovery was possible thanks to the testimony of Humberto Santillán Tabares, who had recently been detained in El Paso during an investigation of the Carrillo-led Juárez Cartel.

The house, two stories high, about 450 feet square, was inhabited by a family that seemed to all appearances completely normal: a mother, father and son. The family had even once invited their neighbors to a small party in their yard. At the same time, however, in the neighborhood of tightly packed houses, there were constant whisperings of strange noises coming from the Tabares's yard, including what once sounded like a shootout. The neighborly gossip was on the mark. The yard where the mother, Érika Mayorga, had once organized a birthday party became the cordoned-off crime scene where investigators found twelve murdered bodies buried in a mass grave. The father of the family, Alejandro García (who worked with Santillán), in order to hide the burials, merely rented a party tent to work behind. When the excavation began in 2004, the bodies were found buried directly on top of one another, indicating that they were assassinated at the same time. Mexican anti-narcotic agents arrested García, along with his wife and son.

The house in the Las Acequias neighborhood became the site of the largest mass grave found in the city, which served as headquarters for the Juárez Cartel. Three bodies were recovered on January 24, 2004, another on the following day and seven more on January 26. All of the corpses were severely disfigured, showing signs of torture, and all were covered in lime, as if the murderers worried that the stink would give them away. Authorities calculated that some of the bodies had been killed and buried only a few days previously. Two of the victims were American citizens. The US Department of Immigration and Customs Enforcement (ICE), with the help of an informant, had been monitoring every step that Santillán had taken in Juárez for months. They had direct knowledge of the murders he had committed but took no action to stop him. The Juárez State Judicial Police, charged by law to investigate the storm of kidnappings and murders, also knew of the hidden grave in Las Acequias, and had known about it since the murder rate had spiked in the city, but failed to act. Perhaps one of the most important revelations to come from the cases against García and Santillán Tabares was not the confirmation that the Juárez Cartel kidnapped, killed and buried people in hidden graves throughout the city, but that the state police both worked in collusion with the cartel and was primarily responsible for some of the kidnappings and murders. The revelation confirmed the long-existing rumor that the cops who patrolled Juárez were not only incapable of solving most crimes but committed those very crimes, working for the cartel as both security agency and assassination squad.

By 2004, officials working for the Juárez Cartel had become known as La Línea (the Line), which was commanded by the Sinaloan Luis Pablo Ríos, known as J.L. Ríos first came to Juárez in 2000 to work as a *pistolero* (low-level gunman) but quickly climbed the ranks to become one of the prime lieutenants of the Juárez Cartel and the possible author of the murders committed in Las Acequias. The unearthing of the bodies in January 2004 was a major blow to the Juárez Cartel. The attorney general, under order of President Fox's PAN government, arrested a large part of the police protective ring—thirteen state policemen in all—and imprisoned them in Mexico City. However, the chief of police, Miguel Ángel Loya Gallegos, who was collaborating with the cartel, escaped and was never seen in the city again. His photograph appeared along with the report of his escape on the front page of *El Diario de Juárez* on January 29, the photo showing the tall and chubby police chief smiling at the scene of a crime. He seemed to look sarcastically toward a victim—a victim he would later become the prime suspect of having murdered.

A photograph of the property of 747 Luna Street also appeared in the same edition of *El Diario*, next to the picture of Loya Gallegos, saying, in effect, that after the unearthing of the bodies in Las Acequias, there were more bodies to be discovered. It was soon after, in February of the same year, that the property of La Rosita was searched again, though with no new discoveries. Despite pressure from the families of the disappeared, the enormous cement block covering the patio was never excavated and remains intact to this day.

3

THE PERFECT PLAN

A persistent honking woke him at about ten in the morning on Friday, May 21. Bright sunlight was bearing down on the gray walls of 5824 Rosita Road.

Vicente pulled himself out of his parents' bed, went into his own room and put on a pair of khaki cargo shorts and a black t-shirt. Little C.E. was still asleep on their parents' mattress, the underside of which was stained with dried blood. Everything, Vicente thought, had gone perfectly the night before. And now Eduardo and Uziel were already waiting for him outside, repeatedly honking the horn of the Cherokee so he would give them the phone card they needed to make the ransom call to his mother's family. His two friends were sticking by him, continuing to help.

Vicente had always been a difficult friend to have. Eduardo and Uziel knew him to be tyrannical, knew that he was crude, that he made fun of everyone around him, but he was also funny and he was always willing to hang out and have a good time. His carefree attitude in front of any authority was contagious: he didn't tuck in his school uniform shirt, he skipped classes, he drank, he got high.

But neither of the two friends would be able to explain how it was that Vicente convinced them to commit one of the most horrendous crimes in the history of one of the most violent cities in the world.

Vicente, however, knew exactly how he had done it. He knew that, without even trying, his friends had always wanted to please him. He figured it was his wits, that he was smarter than the other two, even though his grades were worse. One of the school counselors noticed the same: that he scored among the highest in his class on standardized tests, and yet his grades were at a C average, at best. Even more noteworthy for the counselor was Vicente's response to a survey question about what he would save from his home if there were a fire. His answer: his CDs and stereo. Most of the other students, as expected, said they would rescue their family members. In answer to what he would change about his life Vicente wrote, "I only know that I don't know anything." Next to his answer he drew an open book with question marks on the pages.

In school, one of the few activities Vicente liked and excelled in was reading. On an exam about a text titled "Pretentious-ness," Vicente was able to identify the argumentative method in which it was written, recognizing that it was in third person and used an omniscient and indirect voice. The text—taken from the book *The Profile of Man and Mexican Culture*, by Samuel Ramos—explains that pretentiousness is an attitude developed by people whose capacities are inferior to their ambitions, who thus display superiority in order to cover up internal conflicts. Pretentious persons, according to the author, "are viciously individualistic, unable to understand the values of other people, and reluctant to cooperate." Analyzing the text just months before his murders, Vicente responded that he respects those types of people because pretentiousness "is a style of living for some," and because "some people really do know what they're talking about."

Evidently, he was writing about himself. On the morning of May 21, despite his earlier sketch of a book filled with question marks, he was convinced that he knew exactly what he was doing, that he had committed a perfect crime, that nobody would be able to point to him as the murderer of his family. The only thing left for them to do was report his parents and sister missing. How many murder cases in Juárez, he figured, were never investigated? Who would doubt the story of a teenager living in a family with both a mother and a father (an unusual circumstance for Juárez), who was enrolled and even actively attending school? They might accuse him of being lazy or undisciplined but not of being a serious criminal. To most of his family members and acquaintances, Vicente came off as silent, "normal," even a little shy. It was impossible to detect cruelty in him. Nobody would have seen him as being dangerous. He was among the few children living in Juárez in the beginning of the twenty-first century who actually went to classes; tens of thousands of his contemporaries, mostly because of inadequate and overcrowded classrooms, weren't even enrolled. Vicente was lucky. He lived in a comfortable house on the property his grandfather had passed down to his mother, Alma Delia, when she married his father, Vicente León Negrete. His father, originally from San Cristóbal, Guanajuato, was twenty-four when he married, and it wasn't long before he became the owner of a body shop and auto-painting garage for cars imported from the other side of the border. His father was even able to spend a lot of time at home with his children, as he ran his business from the convenience of his own backyard.

Vicente was also one of the few children in Juárez who grew up with his mother at home. Alma Delia, a third-generation Juárez native—yet another rarity in this city of migrants—decided to be a stay-at-home mom instead of finding work with her business administration degree from the Autonomous University of Juárez. Thousands of children of Vicente's generation mostly raised themselves while their typically single mothers worked long hours in the maquiladoras, trying to make ends meet. There were few affordable daycares or afterschool clubs, and day or night, these children had little more to do but roam the dangerous streets.

The León Chávez family was not just "normal." With both parents present, a spacious three-bedroom house and the kids enrolled in school, they were privileged. And Vicente, so his grandmother described to me in an interview, was just as "normal" as the rest of the family. What problems could he ever get into as long as he was in school?

Vicente's criminal profile, as criminologists would later explain, wasn't necessarily triggered by his emotional shortages or any problems deep within his nuclear family. Rather, they argued that his criminal nature most likely gestated in a wider social circle, in his school, or even in the city itself, where he learned by example that violence was a tool that could solve any number of problems and, perhaps above all else, that those who commit violence, even murder, don't suffer consequences.

He decided that he could easily commit the crime and sell it like an inter-narco settling of scores. After all, he had seen something along these lines just a few weeks earlier, on an afternoon in late April, when a group of armed men stopped by his house, demanding his father do what was expected of all good businessmen in his trade: trick out cars with secret compartments so they can ferry drugs across the border. Vicente heard shouts and screams, followed by the rumble of the armed men driving away in a handful of cars from his dad's shop. To Vicente it was obvious: they were narcos. And it was in this moment, steeped in an adolescent hate for his family, that he understood the key to committing his crime, exactly how he was going to get away with it. It was easy, actually. If he killed them, everyone would automatically think it was a narco crime. And nobody, he was sure, would bother to investigate.

Soon afterward, on an afternoon in early May, during a break in classes, Vicente sat with Eduardo on a bench overlooking a sports field and told him his idea.

"I know how we can make a lot of money," Vicente said, slowing his words, staring fixedly at Eduardo.

"How? You gonna drive a load over the border?"

"No."

"Then?"

"You're probably going to think I'm crazy ..."

"Just say it. What's your plan?"

"I'm going to kidnap someone from my family."

"Who?"

"Who do you think?"

"A cousin ... ?"

"No. My parents."

The answer made Eduardo burst out laughing. Even Vicente had to smile at his friend's reaction.

"You're nuts," Eduardo said.

"Let's move," Vicente responded.

They went to a bench farther away from the other students. From a distance they looked like any two kids talking at recess. It would have been impossible to guess the gravity of what they were discussing.

"But I have it all thought out," Vicente went on. "I know we can pull it off. I'll do the killing, but I need someone else to help me with the ransom." He spoke with a half-smile, noting the expression of disbelief on his friend's face. Eduardo would later claim that he had initially thought it was all a joke.

Their conversation was interrupted when the class bell rang. For a few days they didn't dare mention Vicente's plan again, but when they returned to the idea, they talked about it every single day for two weeks straight, especially after Vicente asked Eduardo about getting a gun and the two of them went to scour the barrios of Juárez.

After repeatedly coming up dry, Vicente found the gun he was looking for in his own school. He got it from a fellow student who'd been in his class since elementary school, though they hardly knew each other and didn't even remember each other's last name. Something about the kid told Vicente that he might have a gun in his house: perhaps it was his cocky gait, or the bravura with which he talked about his family, the power wielded by his father and "his lawyer." The student's name was Alejandro R.A., and he was seventeen years old. Vicente approached him on Wednesday, May 19, during recess and asked him if he had a gun he could borrow, explaining that he wanted to shoot a couple "chumps" who had fought with a cousin of his, nearly giving his dad a heart attack. He made it seem as if Alex was his last chance after asking around in the Melchor Ocampo neighborhood.

Alejandro agreed to get him a gun, and, early the next morning, on May 20, they went to his house, where Vicente watched him walk in the front door and come back out just a few minutes later, carrying a .38 caliber pistol tucked into his waistband. In the middle of the street, in the revealing light of day, Alex handed over the gun, telling Vicente that he'd rent it to him for a thousand pesos. Vicente gave him the money he'd been carrying around for days, which he and Eduardo had saved up together. Taking the gun, he went back to his house, hid it in his room and went to school.

When Vicente saw Eduardo later that day he said that he wanted to talk to him, that everything was ready. Classes ended early that Thursday, around six o'clock, and the boys, using Eduardo's mother's red Dodge Intrepid, drove to Vicente's house in the La Rosita neighborhood. Without his family noticing, Vicente ran into his room and came back out with the gun tucked into his pants. From there the two boys went to the Satélite neighborhood to pick up Uziel, who would later claim that that was the first time he had heard of Vicente's plan. Eduardo, however, would say that Uziel had known what was going on for a few days. What Eduardo and Uziel did agree on in later interviews was that Vicente repeatedly emphasized that the crime needed to be committed with a gun so that it would seem more like a narco crime.

"I'll shoot them while they're sleeping," Vicente said as they drove in the Intrepid, Vicente riding shotgun and Uziel in the backseat.

"The only thing you two need to do is help me drag them out of the house and get them in the car and dump them. Then one of you has to call my grandma and tell her that you have my parents and sister kidnapped and want two hundred thousand dollars for the ransom."

Vicente spoke plainly about the plan, as if he were discussing a group homework assignment and had been elected project leader. The quick succession of events that he described made it seem as though the actual murder wouldn't be difficult, and that the whole thing meant nothing but easy money. $200,000 split three ways would mean 700,000 pesos apiece: each of them could finally afford their own car.

Uziel and Eduardo, doubtful and yet intrigued, listened to their friend. They were somewhere between indecisive and nervous, but Vicente was expecting this, and soon he played his final and most convincing, though simple, hand.

"It's going to look like it was a narco job ... My dad has a lot of enemies. Nobody is ever going to suspect me."

At the very least, all three of them were convinced of that fact. It had only been four months since the city had dug up the mass grave in Las Acequias, and the revealed police involvement in the killings and cover-up became one of the most scandalous headlines in Juárez history. At the same time, the story of the femicides had earned Juárez international fame, giving the impression that the city was as corrupt as it was violent, that officials were incapable of catching murderers or solving crimes. As everyone knew, the cops were working for the cartels, committing both kidnappings and killings, while statistics proved their total inability at issuing justice: of the more than 34,000 reported crimes, police only prosecuted 13 percent. There was also the surging problem of people detained without any proof. The effect of such inefficacy was that victims suffered not only the initial violence of a crime but felt the brunt of a second crime: rampant impunity.

The deaths were enough to convince us of the barbarous state of society, the wave of murder after murder taking the lives of more than 2,500 people since 1993. In just the third week of May 2004, nine people were killed, four of them in narco-style publicly displayed assassinations. On Tuesday, May 18, a man was found riddled with forty bullets from an AK-47 in the parking lot of a Del Río department store next to the city dog track. Just a few hours later, a group of hitmen tried to kill a supposed contact man, Raúl Ortega Saucedo, working between the Juárez and Colombian Medellin cartels. Saucedo would eventually die from his injuries, with the shootout on Abraham Lincoln Avenue in front of the attorney general's office also killing an innocent bystander, a thirty-six-year-old woman and mother. The following day, there was another murder in the western part of the city during yet another standoff between rival gangs. Later, a woman was strangled to death. Finally, and still on the same day, a shoe shiner was shot to death. Not one of the murders would ever be solved.

"Nobody is ever going to investigate," Vicente told Eduardo and Uziel, the three boys still driving around the dusty La Rosita streets.

Though the three friends had grown up in different families and had distinct inclinations when it came to responsibility and the value of human life, there was one thing they agreed on: in Mexico, especially in Juárez, you could commit any crime you wanted and nobody would do a thing about it. About that Vicente was absolutely sure.

"Okay," Uziel said, "if we only have to help you lift them into the car, and then dump them, we'll do it."

"Plus, they're not even our parents," Eduardo added.

Rather than unsettle them, the idea of dumping a few human bodies seemed so simple that it was as though they forgot about having to murder them first. Uziel nodded off in the backseat while Eduardo drove to the house of a girl he couldn't stop thinking about. At around 8 PM, the three boys arrived at the house of S., the eighteen-year-old girl who was the aunt of a friend of Eduardo's and who, when she heard the car pull up, peeked through the window to see Vicente sitting shotgun and toying around with the gun, apparently loading it.

"What the fuck are you looking at?" Vicente asked in typical grace.

"What do you have that gun for?"

"You'll know by tomorrow."

Five feet nine inches tall, thin and fine featured, Vicente gesticulated in such a way that seemed practiced, studied: as if meant to reveal his self-perceived superior intelligence. That was how he answered S., and it was how he answered all women and even how he spoke to his friends, Eduardo and Uziel.

His confidence worked. At his mere order, his two friends killed his parents later that night and dutifully came back to his house the next morning, honking for him to come outside so that they could finish the job.

When Vicente finally stepped hurriedly out the door he saw that one of his father's employees who had arrived for work at 7 AM was polishing a car in the lot.

"Where's your dad, Güero?" the man called.

"Don't know," Vicente responded with his typical indifference. The three friends talked over the plan a few minutes before deciding to go back in the house, where Vicente had a phone card and his grandmother's number scribbled on a sheet of notebook paper. Eduardo and Uziel mentioned that they were planning on going swimming at Las Anitas Water Park later that day.

"You coming?" Uziel asked Vicente.

"I'll try to make it."

"But first," Uziel said, "we should go see if the Explorer is still there."

Vicente agreed, deciding to stay at the house while Eduardo and Uziel went to check on the car. He went into his parents' room and opened the curtains, letting the late morning light stream in through the window. The only person who he considered worthy of his affection was curled up in front of him, still sleeping on the bed. Vicente arranged an electric swivel-fan so that his little brother wouldn't feel the midday heat and then sat down next to him. He felt at peace for the first time in years. He didn't feel nervous or fearful of anybody. He only felt free: finally rid of anyone who could get in the way of carrying out his every fleeting desire. He could never stand when somebody tried to make decisions for him or got in the way of his plans. He didn't believe in rules or laws, nor that someone had the moral authority, or even the genuine intention, to apply the law. His own impulse, from now on, would be his only law.

About twenty minutes later, much sooner than Vicente had expected, Eduardo and Uziel returned. They'd driven to Zaragoza Road and found nothing but the remaining shreds of police caution tape flapping in the wind. The Explorer was gone. State police agents had arrived at 6:20 AM to find the fire in the Explorer already extinguished, the windows exploded, and three unrecognizable corpses in the trunk. Before ten in the morning they had finished collecting the evidence and never considered that two of the murderers would return to the scene of the crime. The two boys weren't worried that they hadn't found the car, but they wanted to know what had happened and decided to buy a newspaper, *El Diario de Juárez*, before heading back to Vicente's house.

"The press still doesn't know," they told Vicente, after scanning the paper. "We can still ask for our ransom before they identify the bodies."

The front page of *El Diario* that morning couldn't have done a better job representing the violence and impunity raging throughout the city. They used only four words, with the banner headline: "Still Unsolved: 23 Executions." The article below identified the sixteen crimes in which twenty-three victims were murdered so far that year, all bearing evidence of having been killed by organized crime. In the fourth paragraph, the text clarified that the number didn't include the twelve bodies discovered in the Las Acequias property. The accompanying photograph was taken at the funeral of Irma Muller, the young mother of three shot to death on Lincoln Avenue in front of the attorney general's office. The image was of a small room filled with people praying; in the background was a casket covered in flowers, partly shadowed by a hanging cross, deftly capturing the horror of a community that would be left defenseless in the coming storm of violence. Even after the discovery of the mass grave, it really wasn't until that Tuesday, May 18, with the reported murder of Muller, whose only "crime" was stopping at a red light at the cross streets of Lincoln and Hermanos Escobar, that the reality of the permeating violence struck the collective consciousness of the city. Muller was murdered for nothing more than being in the wrong place at the wrong time: Juárez, 2004. Her death caused such an uproar that even the young classmates of Muller's three orphaned children took to the streets two days later in a plea for both peace and the prosecution of the murderers. An article about the protest cited Muller's husband, who was as explicit in his analysis as he was ignored: "Just one crime after another, as soon as we finish [mourning] we'll just have to start again. Let's see if we can pressure the authorities enough this time that they finally capture the criminals."

They would not capture them, but not because the authorities didn't know how to investigate. In fact, it was whispered among the top brass in Juárez that there was no such thing as a crime without a lead to unravel. Despite the fact that thousands of murders were left unsolved, police claimed that it wasn't due to incompetency. In 2004, it became clear that when the police weren't the ones actually committing the crimes, or paid or coerced to protect the criminals, they could in fact solve murder cases and even apprehend the criminals. There were always enough clues left behind. The difference between impunity and justice lay in simply following the trail, as soon as possible, even if the victims were burnt to a crisp.

The three friends, Vicente, Eduardo and Uziel, were convinced that after the police found the three bodies in the Explorer, they would do the same thing they did with the thousands of other murder cases in the city: forget about it. Vicente was especially confident. All he had to do was act normal and let the rest of his family know that his parents and sister had disappeared.

"Go ahead and call my grandma," Vicente ordered Uziel

while leafing through the newspaper. "But make sure to use a pay phone."

When his friends left him, Vicente finally woke up C.E., put some sandals on him, scooped him up in his arms, took three hundred pesos from the kitchen table and took off in his undeserving sister's Honda in the direction of his grandparents' house. They lived in the Moreno neighborhood, just a few yards away from the Zaragoza International Bridge. Vicente and C.E., each with a popsicle in hand, walked in and found their grandparents, along with aunts and uncles, eating a late breakfast in the kitchen of the spacious house.

"My parents went out to the movies last night and never came home," Vicente announced to everyone. "They left around eleven with Laura Ivette. C.E. was asleep, so he stayed home with me. I stayed up with some friends until about three, but never saw them come home. They might have left early this morning, I guess ... I was going to go out, but stayed in since they haven't come back yet."

Vicente had his dad's cellphone on him. It rang just as he was telling his grandparents the story. His uncle stood up from the table and, both suspicious and slightly worried, told Vicente he would answer it.

"We have Vicente León and Alma Delia Chávez kidnapped," the uncle heard Uziel say on the other end of the line. "We want two hundred thousand dollars for the ransom."

The Chávez Marquez family were Juárez natives and worked mostly as farm truckers in the Rio Grande Valley. Relatively well off, Vicente's grandfather was able to give his youngest and most adored daughter, Alma Delia, the property where she and her husband raised their family. But despite being close and eating together once a week, the grandparents felt they hardly knew their grandson Vicente.

His story wasn't adding up. How could his parents have gone to the movies at eleven at night if there aren't even movie showings that late? But despite this glaring discrepancy, which they discussed only after their grandson left the house, they decided to call the rest of the family and let them know that Alma Delia and Laura Ivette had gone missing. Vicente had told his grandparents that his dad had a friend who worked for the State Justice Department and could help. Then, with the pretext of calling the friend of his father, he left in search of Eduardo and Uziel to urge them to keep insisting on the ransom money.

The Moreno and Las Anitas neighborhoods are directly next to each other, both cut by the Zaragoza International Bridge and the Rio Grande River, which is close to the water-park where Vicente was soon hoping to meet his accomplices. But Eduardo and Uziel hadn't yet made it to the park. Vicente eventually found them at Uziel's house, in the Satélite neigh-borhood, where they were standing around the Jeep talking.

With a hopeful air, Vicente said, "My whole family knows. They called the police. Now all you need to do is call again and tell them that you're going to kill the hostages because they talked to the cops."

Uziel would later admit to investigators that he went through with his best friend's final instruction without imag-ining the consequences he would suffer.

By six o'clock Eduardo and Uziel were lounging in the pool at Las Anitas Water Park when some of their other friends started to ask about Vicente.

"What makes you so curious?" Eduardo called out from the pool.

"Because we saw him surrounded by a bunch of people," another student responded.

The boys weren't yet alarmed, but they decided to take precautions, Eduardo telling Uziel that they better walk instead of drive back home. Before leaving, however, Eduardo—still looking out for his friend—made sure to leave Vicente's car keys with another friend at the water park.

Taking a shortcut through Zaragoza Road, it can take as little as twenty to thirty minutes to walk from Las Anitas to the Quintas del Valle neighborhood, where Eduardo lived. By the time they were walking home, however, they were already being followed, though nothing the boys did in the following three hours suggests that they had so much as thought of the consequences that awaited them, or the possibility that they might be arrested. Vicente had plotted the crime alone; the other two only agreed to help get rid of the bodies. *He* might get caught, Eduardo and Uziel reasoned, but what did that have to do with them? What really interested them was what a great time they were going to have at the party that night, and the girls who were going to be there, and so when he got home Eduardo changed clothes, hustled back into the Intrepid and drove Uziel to his house, where he waited some twenty more minutes for his friend to get ready for their night out. He thought about calling Vicente, but Vicente beat him to it.

"What's going on? Did they catch you or what?" Eduardo asked as soon as he answered.

"No. Put Uziel on the phone," Vicente ordered.

"Did they get you?" Uziel insisted, without pausing for an answer. "They got you, didn't they?"

"Yes."

"Oh God. Oh God. And now, oh my God, they want to screw all of us over?"

"… Yes …"

Even realizing that Vicente had been caught, Uziel and Eduardo still had little idea of the consequences facing them as accomplices. When Eduardo gave his testimony to the police, it dawned on him that Vicente had been so sure that no one would ever suspect them that he had even started making long-term plans as to what he would eventually do with his parents' land and home. That night, still disbelieving that he would get caught, even after having talked to Vicente, Eduardo tried to concentrate on the girl he had a crush on. He picked her up, and the two of them, along with Uziel, grabbed some hamburgers at a nearby street stand before picking up their other girlfriend, S., who would also later testify to the police. At about 8:30 PM, the group finally made it to the party.

With the love, appreciation and support that Eduardo's family had shown him all his life starting to bloom into something like remorse, Eduardo, dizzy with liquor, began to confess to S. what had happened, albeit in fabrications and half-truths: "Some thugs shot up a friend, and then we shot one of them. We don't know if he's dead or alive," Eduardo told S. on their way home. But he was unable to finish his story. As they were arriving to her house he saw a group of state police officers waiting for him.

The investigation had been relatively simple. The story started to unravel shortly after seven in the morning, when members of the Homicide Investigation Unit, headed by an official of the public prosecutor's office, Jesús Torres Macias, began to collect evidence at the scene of the crime. By that time in 2004, the growing international anger over the forensic mistakes committed during the many femicide investigations had, at the very least, succeeded in applying the necessary pressure to improve forensic analysis, so that the remains of the León Chávez family were recorded in great detail, down to the exact position in which each victim was found and the small bits of charred fabric and other belongings that were lying around them. The first female body, wrote Agent Torres in his report, was found with a fifteen-centimeter-long, two-centimeter-wide piece of knife lodged in her stomach. Another body, the male, was left with his face, legs and arms utterly destroyed by the fire. As with the other two victims, the skull of young Laura Ivette had exploded in the fire. In the truck, the police also found remains of what seemed to be a light-colored, striped bed sheet. There was a black wallet, surprisingly still with an ID card inside—the most important clue found in those first few hours. It read: "Vicente León Negrete. 5824 Rosita Road."

Agent Torres, who led the Homicide Investigation Unit in Juárez until 2005, arrived at the Rosita Road property at two in the afternoon along with two other officers from his team. They entered through the patio, where, in the light of day, they first noticed the parked cars under the metallic awning of the auto shop. Torres also noted stains on the concrete: dark blotches leading to the front door of the house. There were muddied tire prints over one part of the patio, a damp mop leaning against a windowpane. Once in the house they saw the same dun traces of water-thinned blood on the floor. On top of one of the kitchen counters, a knife block was missing three knives. There was blood at the base of the right faucet handle. In the first bedroom visible from the hallway—Vicente's bedroom—there were two pairs of gray pants, one Dickies brand and the other Dockers: Eduardo's and Uziel's school uniforms. The investigators took note of the bloodstains on the walls of the hallway and the doorknob leading to Vicente's room. Their report was so detailed that, in the next hour, Agent Torres would even describe the contours of the shoeprints inside the master bedroom, which seemed to be, he wrote, made by tennis shoes, with both lines and circles in the tracks. Torres reported finding a black piece of plastic that seemed to be a knife handle, as well as traces of blood at the base of the mattress, as well as on the night-stand and on the bed frame in the master bedroom. There was blood spattered on the walls and floor. The standing fan that Vicente had switched on to keep his little brother cool from the merciless Juárez heat had been left on and, as investigators continued their search, continued to swivel left and right. On the patio, Torres even noticed a piece of blue plastic tarpaulin that was torn on one side.

In the midst of his crime scene investigation, Agent Torres received a call from the deputy attorney general's Department of Preliminary Investigations. A family had just reported the kidnapping of three people, one of them with the name of the victim whose ID had been found in the Explorer that morning; the victim's eldest son was starting to sink in a sea of contradictions.

Since he'd left his grandparents' house, Vicente's family had concluded that the teenager was hiding something. When he returned, his cousins and uncles were waiting for him.

"We're going to the police," they said to him.

At that time, the Chihuahua attorney general's office of the

Northern Zone was located on the west side of Juárez on a road named after the famous singer-songwriter Juan Gabriel. It was a run-down two-story building, its offices crammed with dilapidated public prosecutor desks. The Chávez family made their report at the anti-kidnapping unit and, without Vicente's knowledge, his uncles told the agents that they suspected the boy to be somehow involved in the disappearance of his sister. The anti-kidnapping agents contacted the Homicide Investigation Unit, where they already had the name of one of the victims.

"So, Vicente, tell us what happened," the Homicide Unit officer asked the recent orphan.

"Yesterday, at about eleven, my parents went to the movies with my little sister. I stayed home with my brother and went to sleep. When I woke up and realized that none of them had come home yet …"

"Doesn't it seem a little late for your parents to have gone to the movies?" the agent asked.

Vicente could hear the suspicion in the agent's voice. He started acting nervous.

"I don't know …" He was barely able to get a few words out.

"Do you have any issues with your parents, Vicente?"

"No, but my dad has a bunch of problems with some other people …"

The agent stared at him. Vicente began rubbing his hands together.

"Doesn't this all seem a bit suspicious to you?" the agent went on, about to wrap up one of the few homicide cases that would be solved in 2004.

Vicente understood then that nobody believed his story

and that nobody was going to believe it. For some reason (a reason that didn't interest him very much at the moment), his certainty of never being caught gave way, just a little bit, and, in order to push this horrifying realization away, he decided to confess it all, everything, down to the last detail.

"Fine! I can't take it anymore. Me and my friends, we killed them, my parents and my sister."

4

CONSCIENCE

Reporter Armando Rodríguez, known as El Choco (as in "chocolate," in reference to his dark skin), arrived at the *El Diario* newsroom at about 3 PM on May 21, just minutes before our daily briefing. Armando worked the crime beat, and he'd written our banner headline that day about the impunity surrounding the twenty-three cartel murders reported so far that year. Armando loved his job. He loved hard data, and he'd often excitedly share his findings with the rest of the editorial team. Even so, I noticed him unusually animated that day, almost frenetic. Maybe he was feeling that he had just reported on something new, that the violence he was so used to folding into neat statistical boxes—which he had been doing since the mid '90s—had just outgrown its packaging. By 3 PM, Armando knew the identity of the victims found in the Explorer, he knew their home address, their approximate ages and—what had most impacted him—that the family's oldest son had been detained as the prime suspect.

"This sixteen-year-old boy started getting very nervous during his interrogation," Armando said, speaking in his characteristically grave tone and thick Chihuahuan accent.

Like everyone else at the office, the story deeply affected me as soon as I heard the details from Armando. It was the first parricide/fratricide news story I'd ever heard, and what was more, the prime suspect was just a boy.

"And then they had the nerve to go swimming afterward," Armando added, taken aback by the utter disregard for human life.

From his first article on the case—which would be the headline in the following day's paper—Armando reported that the detained teenage suspects had tried to cover their tracks and get rid of evidence, and, quoting Attorney General Óscar Valadez, Armando wrote that it had initially been assumed that the victims were organized crime delinquents who'd been killed in a shootout, which is to say that the triple murder had the effect that Vicente had hoped for: posturing as yet another narco-styled settling of accounts. But the first version of events didn't last very long. That Sunday, May 23, after the attorney general's public relations team interviewed the three boys, a picture of them went viral, along with Vicente's statement that he had killed his parents because, in a nutshell, he believed that they'd always preferred his sister over him and—in his boyish bluntness—because he hated them. Attorney General Valadez told reporters that the teenager showed no signs of regret. Another article published that same day quoted a friend of the León family saying that Vicente had been tremendously jealous when his parents bought his younger sister a car.

Though we didn't yet see what the León family parricide had to do with the larger wave of violence washing over Juárez, many of us intuited that these murders forewarned that the new generation saw narco trafficking and violence as a sort of cloak behind which anyone could run amok, unnoticed, committing any crime they wished; this new generation was willing to kill for the slightest of reasons, or for no reason at all: just because they knew they could. The excavation of the Las Acequias grave and the arrest of police officers who were long involved in the Juárez Cartel seemed to prove to this generation of teenagers that the state couldn't be any more corrupt or any more incapable of enforcing the law. And what else could we expect? What could we expect from a city where corruption had spread to such a degree that, in the past decade, slain bodies were found on a daily basis and investigations were never carried out because many of the authorities actually worked directly for the cartels?

The link between the surge in organized crime and the parricide/fratricide triple murder soon exploded in the press. Meanwhile, the León Negrete and Chávez Márquez families expressed shock and disbelief.

"We don't understand how this happened," Vicente's maternal grandfather said. "They were such a normal family. They'd visit us regularly and never seemed to have any problems. Everything was fine; we don't understand what could've happened."

The León family flew to Juárez from Guanajuato, mistakenly believing their son and his wife and daughter had died in an accident. It was only once they were in Juárez with the parents and brothers of Alma Delia that they found out that their grandson was accused of the murder.

"We didn't know what had happened; they told us there'd been an accident and only after we got here they told us the truth about what had actually happened," said Vicente's paternal grandmother, Consuelo Negrete.

One of the first to point out that the parricide revealed a deep truth about Juárez was a priest named Aristeo Baca. The Juárez priest had already suffered a run-in with Chihuahua's broken justice system during his work as spiritual counselor for the convict Abdel Latif Sharif, known as El Egipcio (the Egyptian), who was arrested for a suspected femicide but who Baca always considered to be innocent. In an interview on Sunday, May 23, Baca argued that the León Chávez murders were proof of the most "vertiginous fall of the values of our city, where violence has eluded the authorities for far too long and where organized crime has surpassed the police's capacity to fight it."

In the days that followed, it was the three teenage murderers who ultimately spelled out the relationship between the generalized lawlessness of the city and the León Chávez murders, when they conceded to separate interviews and, furthermore, gave perfectly believable confessions—a very unusual trait in homicide testimonies in Juárez at that time. Most other murder suspects—in particular femicide suspects —had appeared on camera severely beaten and, for years, had insisted that their confessions had been violently pounded out of them. But Eduardo, Uziel and even Vicente spoke without reservations, both fluidly and candidly, about what they'd done and how the act of murder had seemed so simple to them.

Eduardo was the first of the three boys to be interned at the juvenile detention center, the Escuela de Mejoramiento Social para Menores (School of Social Improvement for Minors, commonly referred to simply as the School), then located in the downtown district of Juárez, on the banks of the Rio Grande. Thanks to his parents, who rushed to verify that he was a minor, Eduardo was tried in juvenile court. He was given five years, the maximum sentence at that time for a minor in the state of Chihuahua.

It was in the School, on Monday, May 24, in one of the social worker's offices, that the seventeen-year-old Eduardo agreed to an interview during which, for the first time, he described how he and his friends had thought the murders would be "easy," and, for the first and last time, he described intimate details of his friendship with Vicente.

"Vicente told Uziel that he'd never get caught," Eduardo said to *El Diario* reporter Pedro Torres, "because he was going to make sure to throw the blame on some people who he said were his dad's known enemies. I think that's why Uziel thought it would be easy, and since I wasn't going to be directly involved [in the murders] ... I thought something like, 'Well, they aren't my parents, so why should I care?' ... But I should've thought about it more, because they were still two human beings, and no one deserves to die, and definitely not in that way ... Vicente told us we wouldn't have anything to do with murdering them or anything like that, that we wouldn't be directly involved, that the only thing we were going to do was ditch the bodies somewhere and call his grandparents for him and ask for the ransom."

Dark-skinned, thin and not quite as tall as Vicente (though taller than Uziel), Eduardo responded easily to the questions posed by the reporter, who wrote that the teenager kept his gaze fixed on the ground during the entire interview. Among other things, Eduardo described Vicente as a manipulator, but acknowledged that he couldn't seem to push him away. "He's a guy who likes to be all laid back and everything, but when there's a problem or something he leaves you on your own, so you have to handle things however you can. He likes to be right. If you have an opinion about something and he also has one, he always thinks he's right, and if you make a mistake, he'll make fun of you or say something like, 'Ah, you're such an idiot,' or something like that. And if he is right, then he always says, 'See bro, what the fuck are you even talking for if I'm always the one that's right' … I'm only now realizing that he has this way of influencing people, of roping you into his plan, of convincing you. I mean, he has this way of making you feel that nothing bad will ever happen to you," Eduardo said.

"Do you still consider the other two your friends?" the reporter asked.

"Uziel, I do. We had more in common. He seems like a better person to me than Vicente because I could see that he wanted to do something with himself. He was older and was still in school, he wanted to try hard, he didn't want to flunk anymore, and things like that. I saw him with clearer goals for himself … but now I guess those goals are a little more unclear."

The possibility of being arrested for committing a crime of that magnitude did briefly pass through his head, Eduardo admitted in the interview, but then the idea simply vanished. "If I would've known, if I could've seen the consequences I was going to face, seen what my family was going to suffer, I think that would've completely stopped me, but I only needed a little push to stop myself, and I think that that little push never came, and that's why all this happened."

By the standards of Juárez, Eduardo, too, had a wholesome family life. His father provided for the kids with his maquila job and his mother took care of the house. Though Eduardo had dual nationality and could have studied in El Paso, his family, as a sort of prize for his good behavior, let him enroll in Juárez schools, where he wanted to be. Both parents had already visited him twice since he'd been interned at the juvenile detention center, where they'd reiterated their love and support for him, advising him to accept the terrible deed he'd done, serve his sentence and ask God for forgiveness. Only in this way, his pained parents explained to him, could he live out his sentence with his head held high. Despite his parents' understanding, Eduardo was still terribly overwhelmed by guilt. He felt that, above all, he'd let them down and that they would forever live with the tragic burden of having raised a son who was a murderer. The only time during the interview that Eduardo broke into tears was when he said to the reporter that he felt he hadn't been able to talk in earnest with his parents, that he hadn't had the time to tell them how much he loved them and that he hoped someday, if they could find it in their hearts, they would forgive him for what he'd done. And even more than the pain he felt for his parents, Torres wrote, Eduardo showed great emotional distress for how his crime and arrest would affect his little brother.

"I always tried to look after him. I always cared about what he was up to, where he was, but now I don't know what he's feeling at all. I love him so much and I hope that one day he can forgive me too, but if he wants to deny me as his brother, then of course, that's his right, because I don't know what I would do if I were in his place."

The interview with Eduardo was published Tuesday, May 25, in *El Diario*, the same day that, along with Pedro, I interviewed Vicente in the adult prison center, El Centro de Readaptación Social para Adultos de Juárez (Juárez Social Rehabilitation Center for Adults). Above all, I wanted to ask the young parricide two things: How is it exactly that a teenager gets his hands on a gun in this city? And how was it that murdering three people—without even mentioning the fact that they were his own family members—and driving an unregistered car with three dead bodies in the backseat had seemed "easy" to him? Didn't he think anyone would arrest them?

The jail was next to the military base at the southwestern edge of the city. It was a ramshackle, dirty building that housed more than 4,000 inmates piled into cells with only half that capacity. More than 1,000 heroin addicts were detained there, and the place was often known as "the biggest drug-lounge of Juárez." But the prison was still relatively calm considering the storm that would come in the next few years: deadly fight after bloody brawl ravaging the prison corridors. In those "peaceful" years, the gang members of Los Aztecas, Los Mexicles and Los Artistas Asesinos (the Assassin Artists) could still share a courtyard.

Vicente was held at the adult prison because no one had bothered to bring his birth certificate to prove he was a minor. The nearly two weeks that it took for his public defender, Jorge Gonzalez, to send and process the document Vicente spent living in Ward 16. Getting approved for an interview with him was only a matter of asking at the prison entrance. I was able to meet with him in an administrative office at eleven the same morning. The first thing I noticed when he came in was that, though it was four days after his detention, he was still wearing the same black shirt and khaki Bermuda shorts he'd been wearing in photos taken the previous Saturday. Not one of his family members had taken the time to send him clothes. Later, I'd find out that no one in his family would ever try to contact him again.

Thin, with closely cropped hair, Vicente was the tallest of the three teenage murderers. He was wearing the orange polyester vest that inmates wear when they're taken to court or an administrative office on the grounds. With a firm, seemingly calm look on his face, he sat on one of the office benches, waiting for my questions. He put a hand to his chin as soon as I started to ask him how and when he had first thought of his crime, to which he responded, as to all my other questions, coldly, candidly, and in precise details about his actions and motivations.

"I'd asked [my parents] if I could go to this party that was coming up on a Friday night. They told me I could go. Then, that Tuesday, I reminded them, and again they said I could go. Wednesday too, and they said yes, and it went on like this until Friday. That day I took a shower and changed and as soon as I told my dad that I'm leaving he tells me, 'Where you going?' And I say, 'You know, to the party, remember I've been asking about it since Monday?' He said, 'No, no, you can't go.' 'But you already told me I could. Why not now?' 'Because I don't want you to. And you're not going.' Then we got in a fight and my mother got involved, saying that I always wanted to have it my way, and she was definitely on my dad's side, and then both of them started to yell at me. I got so angry, I went to my room and got in bed and cried and, I don't know, then I got the idea, just like that, out of the blue, that I hated them.

"The next day at school I told Eduardo my plan. He was weirded out. At first he thought it was a joke, but we talked a while and he could tell that I was serious and he told me that I knew what I was doing and that I could count on him. I think he thought that if he didn't have my back that I'd just do it anyway. And I don't know if he was trying to keep on my good side, or maybe he thought that if he said no to me, we'd fight. So he said yes.

"First it was only a plan to kidnap them, but since we didn't know what to do exactly, and we couldn't come up with anything, I suddenly thought, what if we kill them? Since then, we almost always talked about the plan.

"We told Uziel later. He suspected something was up because he'd look at me and Lalo strangely and we weren't hanging out with him anymore. Then Uziel asked me what was up with us, and I told him everything. We were outside my house, on the back patio, and I told him the plan, that we were going to try to murder my parents and make it seem like a kidnapping. At first, Uziel was even more freaked out than Eduardo, and he told me to think everything through really well. He didn't say anything to us at first, until the next day, or maybe two days later, and he said that, yeah, I probably knew what I was doing, that they were my parents and that he'd help me out too. That's when we really started to plan things.

"The first thing we decided was that we had to do it with a gun. That was because, since my dad had so many enemies who were narco traffickers or the police, it had to be with a gun so that it would look like an execution. My dad had a car shop, he also owed people money, and he had some problems with some narcos who came by the house one day with AK-47s. It was so obvious what was happening. They came, they fought, they took a lot of cars, and then they left."

How did you actually get the gun?

"Eduardo and I went to the Melchor Ocampo neighborhood thinking that we could, I don't know, talk to some thugs and ask around until we found someone who could get it for us. Eduardo stole 1,600 pesos from his dad's wallet, but when we went looking we didn't come up with anything until finally a friend from school lent us one … His name's Alejandro, or Alex. We went to elementary school together."

What's Alex's last name?

"I don't remember … but here, I got it written on my shirt."

Vicente stood, lifted his orange vest and pulled up his t-shirt, revealing barely legible words written in pen on the underside of the shirt.

Alejandro Ruiz Escareña?

"No, this one … starting with R, I think …"

Alejandro R.A.?

"Yeah, that's Alex. He lent us the gun."

"But before we went through with it there was some trouble at my house. My dad had a heart attack, and since we were out looking to find a gun that same day [Vicente started to smile, covering his mouth with a hand] … I remember Eduardo teasing me, saying, 'Look, he's gonna beat us to it.' At first I even felt a little bad, but then I told myself, 'If I'm out looking for a gun to kill them, I mean, why do I feel bad?' And then I got over it.

"My dad had a heart attack because he found my sister with her boyfriend, and he yelled at her, and smacked her around, and even though he knew he shouldn't get so upset because he'd already had a heart attack and was predisposed to have another, I think he overdid it, and that's what gave it to him."

What was it that finally made you decide to kill them?

"I think it was hate, then greed. First I just wanted to free myself from them, but then I said to myself, 'If we're going to do it, we might as well get something out of it as well,' and that's when we thought of kidnapping them to get some money."

Eduardo said that you convinced them that it would be really easy. What made you think it would be so easy? Didn't you think the police would arrest you?

"We really thought it was a perfect plan. It's just that we never [he tapped a finger on his head] even thought that the police existed. Never. Not once did we worry about them. We thought that they'd find the bodies, ask some questions maybe, and then that would be it, everybody would forget. We never thought to ask, 'What if they found us out? Or what if they caught us?' We told ourselves, 'We're in Mexico, a corrupt country, the cops are only decoration.' I mean, we saw Mexico as completely corrupt, full of impunity, you know, like how many cases … like the deaths of women here in Juárez, I mean, how many are there? Like four hundred or something. We thought that the cops were just there for show. If a cop catches you in a club or on the street with a bag of coke, or pot, or any drug, you think right away, 'I'll hand over two, three hundred pesos, whatever I have on me, and they'll let me go. If I run a red light, I give fifty pesos to the traffic cop and that's it.' I mean, we thought the laws were there to be broken. That's why they're there.

"What we did has no justification, no forgiveness. I know that everybody sees me now as the worst person in the world, and that's what I am, I even hate myself, and if there were a pistol here I would grab it and kill myself right now, or maybe,

I don't know, I wouldn't even kill myself, I would try to suffer as much as I could first, and then I would kill myself."

Prison doesn't seem like enough punishment to you?

"No, they're saying that since I'm a minor the most they're going give me is five years, which is a joke even to me. I mean, according to the law my family is only worth five years? If I was outside looking at me in here, I'd be for killing me."

The interview was published on the front page of the Wednesday, May 26, edition of *El Diario* with the headline "We Didn't Think the Police Would Investigate." The article generated various reactions and opinions over who was most to blame for both the murders and the popular perception that there are no consequences to crime: the teenager devoid of feelings and values, the family that never taught him those values, the state that does nothing to arrest criminals, or the media that ceaselessly reports on lawlessness and acts of violence.

Shamelessly, without remarking on the profound cynicism the statement evoked, the police themselves were the first to come out and say that the triple murder committed by the three teenagers was a consequence of the impunity running rampant in Juárez: "The minors who committed the multi-homicide exhibited what can only be called an 'awareness of impunity,' which developed after years of rising insecurity and inadequate crime scene investigation in the city. We've endured years of backwardness, which the authorities should take note of," explained Chief of Police Ramón Domínguez Perea, in charge of public safety for the local PAN government. "This awareness of impunity," Perea continued, "permeates society to such a degree, as we have seen in the case of Vicente León Chávez, that people think they can commit crimes without facing any consequences at all. And so it's necessary that we make sure that the media is up to date, that they know that the different branches of government do coordinate with each other and share information in a way that has achieved results, like we have seen today in this case, as well as, more generally, in the societal results reached in other cases."

The coordination that Domínguez mentioned was the *Comprehensive Plan for Public Security*, the first attempt to establish increased communication between the three branches of government, which President Vicente Fox was pressured to implement. First presented to the public in 2003 by State Secretary of Chihuahua Santiago Creel, the plan included a number of objectives, including firing and prosecuting police officers with connections to organized crime, a goal that would fail to be addressed at every level of government.

In 2004, the official in charge of implementing the *Comprehensive Plan* was Héctor González Valdepeña, commander of a police force then known as the Federal Preventive Police Unit, who, when interviewed about Vicente's crime, agreed with Police Chief Perea in identifying the "number one enemy" in Juárez.

"It's impunity," Chief Perea admitted. "The idea that anything goes. In the end it's like this: of the many crimes committed, very few are solved, and so people think just like those kids. And though it's a shame that such a young kid recognizes this impunity, I don't think it's the only factor that drove him to commit such a terrible crime. There are other reasons, but it's obvious that he thought there wouldn't be any consequences, at least not any real consequences." Valdepeña added that he felt "worried that more and more people could begin to think that there is complete impunity, coming to the conclusion that they can commit any crime they want."

The heads of both the state and city police forces coordinating the public security plan spoke so openly about the failure of the Juárez justice system that they seemed not to even recognize that they themselves were integral links in the chain of command responsible for that failure. If Vicente's comments cut to the core of the problem, the chiefs' responses reflected the common practice of punting the blame to someone else.

When the public prosecutor's office was asked about its own responsibility in creating the generalized perception of impunity in Juárez, the spokesperson for the deputy attorney general, Mauro Conde, claimed that it was the media's fault for showcasing nothing but negative stories about the police, thus leading people like Vicente to think they could get away with murder. "Without wanting to point any fingers," Conde said, "it's the media's fault because people only ever hear about the bad things that happen, and the many cases that are solved never get as much attention as the violent crimes. This current case, for example, has been in the news for over a week, and surely it's going to stay in the headlines even longer. But if, after an investigation, another culprit is caught, sure it might get reported on, but it's not going to stay in the news very long at all."

In an op-ed published on May 30 titled "Consciousness of Impunity," *El Diario* argued that the teenagers' crime should spark a period of reflection for everybody living in the borderlands: "How many people in a similar situation would commit a grave crime, if they had the firm belief that at the end of the day nobody was going to care and he or she would be left ignored and unpunished? This should be a call for each of us to think deeply about what is going on in our community, to reconsider our conception of the model family, the role that education plays in childhood development, the lessons we are teaching the next generations, the environment we are creating for our children, how we interact with the media, the government, community organizations and even the church. In the end we need to ask: what has happened to our society that we must witness the cold-hearted murder of a family by one of its very own members?"

An answer to the first of the two questions would come just a few days later, on June 2, in Vicente's high school, Colegio de Bachilleres 6, when a student nearly stabbed a fellow student to death. During a brawl that erupted in the school, the aggressor, in the plain light of day, took out a knife and sank it into his classmate's chest.

At the time, Juárez was in the middle of an election cycle for both state and city government. José Reyes Baeza and Héctor Murguía, members of the historically dominant PRI party, were leading in the polls (though only 30 percent of the population would vote in the local elections), with both candidates completely removed from the reality of life in the city. The article on the school stabbing was hidden among election trifles as well as a note on the construction of a new maquiladora, Electrolux, which would "detonate" the urban growth of another huge swath of land in southeast Juárez.

An *El Diario* reader wrote a letter to the paper saying that she was "profoundly impacted" not only by Vicente's crime, but by society's incapacity to see itself reflected in it. She explained that she decided to write her letter after overhearing a conversation in which two of her coworkers referred to Vicente as a "thankless, poorly raised son-of-a-bitch," and a "crazy psychopath" who deserved to die and should not be forgiven. She wrote: "I felt uncomfortable to the point of not understanding why, and so I started analyzing what was bothering me. And then I remembered that at Vicente's age I also, at various times and in different ways, wanted to disappear my parents, who beat me, who forced me to work, who mistreated me emotionally and often told me that I wasn't worth anything. And yet there was something in me that stopped me from taking any action against them, something that Vicente didn't have, and which I can now identify and perfectly relate to. I don't know his background, but in his face I see sadness, hate, depression, and rage. I'm not justifying what he did, and I recognize that he committed a heinous crime, but I know that he was in deep need of attention and affection, just like I was at his age. Today I thank God that I didn't do anything to my parents, and I'm thankful for the therapy that helped me and spoke to me and took away my pain, a therapy that Vicente didn't have. I beg our community to look beyond the basic facts and try to understand this young man, to examine his conscience, and to ask ourselves how our own children are doing, if we're abusing them, whether physically or emotionally. Whatever answer we come to, we have the chance to change our ways, to look for help and to stop the abuses and prevent another crime sparked by hate. I believe that, as members of this society, we share a responsibility, and that we owe it to these three young men to do more than merely judge, criticize and condemn."

The day after giving their interviews, Vicente and Uziel received their sentences in the Second Penal Court under Judge Catalina Ochoa. In each of their cases, Ochoa decided that they were guilty of parricide (in Mexican law, parricide is distinguished from homicide by longer terms of punishment) and premeditated homicide exhibiting "brutal ferocity" to kill Vicente León Negrete, Alma Delia Chávez and the minor Laura Ivette León Chávez. For Uziel, the judge explained that although he wasn't an actual relative to the victims, he was charged with parricide because "he knowingly participated in the murder of persons he knew to be the family of Vicente León Chávez." Explaining her term "brutal ferocity," the judge added that the condemned, "given the details of the murders," displayed "a complete disregard for human life."

The next day *El Diario* published a photograph of the two boys behind bars at the hearing: Vicente, who was still wearing the same black t-shirt a week later, seemed to be listening with indifference while Uziel looked on at the judge's secretary with the same expression of anguish and panic that he had had during his interviews. As the only legal adult of the three boys, Uziel faced the longest jail time. With the reforms inspired by the judicial fracas surrounding the femicides, he could face up to sixty years in prison, as two of his victims were women. The recent change in law could derail his entire life in a matter of minutes.

On that same Wednesday, May 26, Alejandro R.A., the boy whose name was written on the underside of Vicente's shirt, along with his lawyer, came to find me at my *El Diario* office. They waited for me at the reception desk, the lawyer claiming to have represented the R.A. family for the past two years. I showed them to my cubicle on the top floor of the newsroom, where I set a recorder between us and listened to what Alejandro had to say.

"They [Vicente, Eduardo and Uziel] told me that they had gone to different neighborhoods looking for a gun, and they came over to my place too, but I never lent them anything," Alejandro began, though he was almost immediately interrupted by his lawyer.

"Do you have any guns in your house?" the lawyer asked Alejandro, as if he were questioning a witness in court.

"No."

"Then," the lawyer continued, "why do you maintain that you didn't lend them anything?"

"Because, for starters, I don't have any guns. I don't get involved in those kinds of things, and also I wasn't about to try to help them get one."

Alejandro went on to describe how the articles written by *El Diario* were causing him trouble in school, and that the principal even took him to his office to ask him if he'd had anything to do with Vicente's case.

"That's what the principal was saying to me, practically interrogating me to see if I had any guns, and so I told him, 'You know what, I don't have any guns. If you want, you can talk to my mom and she can bring in a lawyer to solve this problem.'"

"Furthermore," the lawyer interjected, "the name of my client doesn't appear in any of the police reports."

"How do you know what's in the police reports?" I asked.

"That's confidential."

I would later learn that in 1999 that same lawyer who was representing Alejandro at my desk, Ignacio Esqueda, had defended the owner of the La Campana Ranch and "the bunker" in the La Rosita neighborhood where six bodies were discovered, marking what would be a new era of violence in Juárez.

5

IMPUNITY

Human skin turns the color of lead as the body loses blood. It's one of the physical signs, perceivable at plain sight in a homicide victim, marking the boundary between life and death. Another is the color of the blood itself, from the almost translucent, still glistening red of those recently massacred, to the blackening brown of bodies found long after death. The skin of victims murdered by bullet or blade turns ashen at the same pace as their blood drains from the wounds, fanning out from the body. Ambient temperature can slow or speed this process. Heat accelerates the chemical breakdown of blood, the rate at which it loses color and becomes more viscous once it is outside the body. The body, meanwhile, slowly inflates like a wrinkled balloon. The blood also leaves a brown, almost impossible to remove stain on sidewalks, streets, floors, walls. Family members tend to cover these stains with sand, others try to wash them away with a hose, literally smearing blood across the city streets.

The most horrifying moment for families tends to be when the body is removed from the scene of the crime, when the victim is stripped and the bullet entry and exit points are exposed, perfectly round and rimmed by the black burn of gunpowder soot that contrasts against the color of skin.

But the barbarity of the crime is most palpable in the sheer lifelessness of the bodies left on the ground, sometimes found lying on their sides, their hands over their bellies, their shoulders and legs torn apart by the impact of each bullet, or sometimes they're still bleeding or, if they were shot in the head, their faces can be almost completely obliterated—this is how they drop by the thousands, without explanation.

In the vast majority of cases, knowing the motivating factors behind each crime has been the exclusive privilege of the murderers. For the families of the victims, and for the community at large, there are only leads—leads that always fall short.

In 2004, the administration of President Fox announced the plan to improve criminal investigations, as part of a larger judicial reform financed by the United States with the intention of introducing Juárez to the "adversarial" system of oral court proceedings. By 2010, the plan had been reduced to a system of police, forensic experts and public prosecutors who were only able to present evidence and probable suspects in 3 of every 100 homicide cases throughout the city, a ratio that dipped even lower than before the reform. Of the other 97 out of 100 crimes, it was officially filed that there was no evidence and there were no leads to follow.

In these years, marked by the violence attributed to a turf war between two cartels—which coincided with the introduction of the new justice system—the authority of public officials sank woefully, along with their performance indicators. Between 2008 and 2010, a period in which more than 7,000 people were found murdered in Juárez and the city became the most violent in all of Mexico, evidence against alleged suspects was found in less than 200 cases. In the other 6,800 cases, only trace remains were left behind to piece together how or why each murder was committed. The public prosecutor's office actually stopped surveying crime scenes altogether, and over the course of six years—from 2004 to 2010—it was a rare sight to see police officers patrolling the more dangerous neighborhoods. That left all fieldwork to forensic investigators, the only officials who contributed evidence to preliminary investigations or case files.

In contrast to the cases from the '90s, the new case files were only recording who or what led to the finding of each victim, the position of the body found on the ground—decubitus, in forensic terminology—the physical characteristics (hair and skin color, complexion, clothes) and copious amounts of details of the necropsy, such as the exact entry and exit point of each bullet, the trajectory of the bullet through the body and all the damage caused en route, including organ lacerations and bone fractures. Each wound left behind a detailed record, even if the victim had more than a hundred bullet wounds.

The lead investigators were also meticulous in detailing the shell casings found at the scene of the crime; they counted them and organized them by caliber—useful to determine how many guns and how many shooters were present. A database from the assistant attorney general's office compiled more than 1,000 homicide cases and found that at least one-fourth of the crimes committed during 2008 were committed with 9-millimeter handguns. AK-47 machine guns took second place.

And that's it.

In the vast majority of cases no one looked for more leads or witnesses to the murder; no one questioned anyone but the immediate family members, and that was almost always done to know one thing and one thing only: what did the victim do for a living? If there was any reason to believe that the victim had, at any point in their lives, direct or indirect contact with any aspect of narco trafficking, then the public prosecutor's office would try to establish which criminal group could be implicated and then close the case. The case files showed no evidence of further questions and detailed no other interviews. The victim was somehow caught in the line of fire, and so they died. Who killed them and why? That was the least of the state's concerns. They were somehow involved, period. End of investigation. Even though, in many cases, there were eyewitnesses. During the length of an entire presidential administration, the agents of the public prosecutor's office didn't do anything beyond stacking case file upon case file until there were thousands, all of them filled with nothing but the most basic forensic analyses.

With 97 percent of the cases lacking all explanation aside from the acknowledgment that, yes, there was indeed a narco war going on, and with a state that used that acknowledgment as an excuse to evade its responsibility in carrying out justice, we Juárenses lived without the support of evidence to help us understand the extraordinarily complicated phenomenon of the skyrocketing rate of violent crime. In Juárez, murder was the end of a life, as well as its own explanation. Our lack of understanding reduced the gravity of the annihilation of a human life to a summary, to a statistic, to one more slot added to the file cabinet of case files. It was as if murders were committed not by individuals who ran the streets, or by the caliber of their weapons, but by an unexplainable and lethal shadow that was passing over the city.

Judicial impotence served as a mirror held up to the face of the barbaric society that we had become: our highest ideals were a privately operated justice system and the right to commit any crime we wanted. It was as if we had returned to the pre-civilized state of man, to utter lawlessness. But there *were* existing laws; they just weren't being enforced. Indeed, the penal code of Chihuahua State begins by explaining that the purpose of each and every investigation is to "establish the truth, guarantee justice in the application of our laws and resolve conflicts and crimes, in order to contribute to the restoration of social harmony." The rule of law also claims that the state's greatest responsibility is to protect the individual, even more than protecting the state itself.

The Vicente León case showed us that thorough investigation is the only way for us to get close to the root cause of a crime, to that explosive combination of personal motivations and social factors gestating in every person who decides to commit murder. Although we could generate theories, speculate and even pass public policies that attempted to explain or combat crime, without appropriate investigations shining light on the cascade of murder cases, it was impossible to know what was actually going on. We needed justice to understand and resolve the phenomenon of violence taking place throughout Mexico. In the state of impunity in which we lived, we could only imagine or catch glimpses of the monstrous consequences of violent crime, and it was only a matter of time before our indifference to the flood of homicides finally turned into a pervasive sense of insecurity and fear. Because we were never able to know who the murderers were, we felt that anyone and everyone could have blood on their hands. Of whom, we asked ourselves, with increasing exasperation, should we be scared?

Vicente, who was so convinced that no one would ever investigate his crime, was paradoxically one of the very few persons detained for murder in Juárez in 2004—a year in which leads were found in less than half of homicide cases, most of which were said to be a result of inter-cartel fighting. And it just so happened that one of the driving motives behind the boy's triple murder had been the very perception that hardly any crimes in the city were investigated. Though he had publicly confessed to killing his family because he hated his parents for preferring his sister, the criminologists at the Juárez Social Rehabilitation Center for Adults argued that whatever triggered his crime had little to do with the goings-on of his nuclear family. Rather, the trigger had been "exogenous"—they wrote in Vicente's case file when he arrived at Cereso prison—it came from outside the home, perhaps from his school, his neighborhood or even the city at large. Vicente's psychological character was officially classified in the case file as 2004/1338, that is: "lacking socialization with a tendency toward distortion at the moment of internalization and interjection of social norms." The specialists came to that conclusion in his interview shortly after he was first admitted in May 2004, when he told them, as he'd told me, that he had been sure that no one would investigate the murder of his family or try to find him, that he knew as well as anyone else that the city and federal police forces were corrupt, that they themselves were killing people and no one was doing anything to stop them. Ada Robles, lawyer and expert on the Juárez cartel, who for fifteen years was chief of the Cereso prison's Department of Criminology, understood the boy's motives to be his personal interpretation of the sociocultural makeup of his city and country. It was his way, the criminologist argued, to say: "Why can't I? Why should you punish me if our whole society is rotten? What do you expect? Why shouldn't I kill [my family] if women are getting killed around me every single day?"

Vicente had made that assessment of Juárez back in 2004, when the homicide rate was around 300 per year. My interview with Robles was years later, in 2011, when the yearly murder rate was in the thousands. The perceived lack of punishment, Robles said to me with well-founded pessimism, has multiplied a thousand-fold. "That is inevitably guiding our youth. They say to themselves: 'What is going on? I can rob a cashier and nothing is going to happen to me. By the time they arrest me, I'll have already spent the money and come and gone I don't know how many times.' Because, unfortunately, this is the type of society that impunity creates."

An analysis of the Juárez femicides, published in 2010 by the Catalonia Office for Peace and Human Rights, argued that the "institutionalized apathy toward the murders" is itself a mechanism for structural violence that trivializes attacks on the community and, through its constancy, naturalizes and normalizes acts of aggression.

Vicente was the first person in whom I'd seen this idea played out firsthand. He seemed to have a unique reaction to the violent crime rate: instead of anger, fear or dismay, what was actually bubbling up inside him was a profound disregard for human life. "Mexico is corruption," he said. "The police are just decoration." And he was right.

That year of 2004 in Juárez, just as in the rest of the country, there was a generalized conviction that the police and justice system could not be more corrupt or inefficient. The whole world seemed to know this. Chihuahua was the international paragon for exuberant incompetence when it came to finding evidence that would lead to suspected murderers. The Las Acequias scandal served as a straightforward indictment because it unveiled a link between identifiable officers and identifiable victims, but it wasn't the first piece of evidence tying Juárez police to organized crime. Historic examples abounded, implicating all levels of government. In 2000, for example, a group of municipal police officers was linked to the release of a suspected narco trafficker and an entire ton of marijuana conveniently caught mid-shipment but then rerouted back to the narco trafficker. Even as far back as the '90s it was reported that Federal Judicial Police Commander Elias Ramirez Ruiz had ties to Rafael Muñoz Talavera, the nephew and confidante of drug lord Rafael Aguilar. An even older case was that of Javier Coello Trejo, a prosecutor working for the Unit of Investigations and Reform Against Narco Trafficking under President Carlos Salinas de Gortari, who in April of 1990 visited Juárez to unveil the new "punishment by up to thirty-five years in prison for any police officer proven to have ties to narco trafficking." Four years later Coello himself was charged in a Texas court case for receiving expensive gifts in exchange for the protection of Juan García Abrego, the head of the Gulf Cartel.

The Drug Enforcement Administration summarized in a 1998 report presented to the US Senate: "There is no Mexican institution of law enforcement that the DEA can entirely confide in."

"In Mexico, the narcotrafficking mafias are more powerful

than ever before, and the level of corruption in that country cannot be equaled in any other part of the world," testified DEA Administrator Thomas Constantine.

Oscar Maynez was the criminologist heading the public prosecutor's office's Department of Expert Witness Services. In 2002, he resigned because of internal disagreements surrounding the investigation of eight women found slain in a cotton field. When I questioned him in 2004 about the involvement of police in the Las Acequias mass grave, he said it was clear that government corruption was the only sound explanation for the control that narco trafficking had over Mexico. "For organized crime to exist," he said, "it must have 'officialized' protection." I interviewed him in front of his class at the Institute of Social Sciences and Administration at the Autonomous University of Juárez. Sarcastically, Maynez asked his students how much they knew about the twelve bodies found at Las Acequias, where, "Hold on to your seats," he said to them, "it seems that police were involved." The students responded with a collective cry of irony, "Naaah! How strange is that!"

The national and international condemnation of how organized crime had infiltrated Chihuahua's justice system was nothing compared to the international upheaval about how the femicide crimes were being handled. Three hundred and seventy-eight women were reported murdered in Juárez between 1993 and 2004. With mounting international pressure, President Vicente Fox created a federal prosecutorial team that, by January 2004, had made headway in only twenty-one cases, while another sixty cases with preliminary investigations had proved "impossible to follow up on." It seemed no one was willing to conduct a serious investigation.

In the ingrained system of impunity of the '90s, there developed several social, political and media-related phenomena. Local feminist organizations cropped up in defense of women's rights and demanded justice for the murder victims of gender crimes. Thanks to their efforts, information about femicides soon started circulating both nationally and internationally. Within a few years it seemed that the entire world had an opinion about these cases. A 2005 article published in *El Diario* estimated that the femicides had, since 1999, been the main topic of at least eighteen books, twelve plays, nine feature-length films and documentaries, fourteen songs and a myriad of reports from various national and international media outlets, particularly from Europe and the United States. There were even multiple analyses of the various femicide theories: how each explained, interpreted and presented Juárez as a world capital of violence against women.

The theses were as diverse as their authors. One investigation, by Erin Frey, professor of history at Yale University, found three main narratives in the various artistic, commercial and journalistic mediums covering femicides in 2008: the first understood the murders to be a result of neoliberal politics and its injustices, the second drew a relationship between the murders and impunity and the failures of government to protect women, and the last argued that they were simply individual acts committed by one or more serial killers in the city. Not one of them examined the problem of violence in all its aggregate complexity, and all of them, Frey concluded, examined the femicides through the lens of gender. Frey added that the three theories failed to consider that the violence of Juárez was not only targeting women but men as well, and in much greater numbers. She demonstrated this via a database from the Colegio de la Frontera Norte (Northern Border University) comparing the number of murdered men to murdered women between 1985 and 2004. A total of 378 women were reported murdered between 1993 and 2004. In the same time span, 2,700 men were reported murdered.

By 2004, the kaleidoscopic narrative that had formed around the femicides had spurred hours upon hours of interviews with the victims' families, especially the mothers of the victims, who seemed to suffer a little more with each question they were asked. There was a deep disconnect characterized by the masses tuning into local, national and international coverage and the painful sense of alienation, impotence and impunity in which these mothers were living. They shared with the media stories of their loved ones being killed over one, two, three, sometimes even six years without seeing any results and without seeing any justice. How were we to understand this epidemic of murder and violence? What else did we need to witness in Juárez to comprehend the severe lack of justice consuming the mothers and families of the thousands upon thousands of homicide victims?

It was at this critical point that the León Chávez family paid for the impunity suffered by other families with their own blood. It was at this critical point that Vicente became the first murderer whose case was seen as direct evidence that crime was contaminating us all, and that impunity, which we had understood as an unfortunate grievance for the victims, was in reality a problem for all of Juárez: impunity had taught us that any and every savage crime was fair game.

6

THE SYSTEM

On the morning of January 6, 2005, six men shuffled nervously in the small holding cell* of the Seventh Sentencing Court in the San Guillermo State Prison of Chihuahua City. The judge ordered them to silence and they froze like recently captured animals—sacrificial lambs—trapped in the courtroom cage; they had just heard their sentencing of up to forty years in prison for the murder of six women. Suddenly, a rough voice rose above the din, spitting out legal terms, claiming that their rights had been violated. José Luis Rosales Juárez, a twenty-eight-year-old Zacatecan who had been raised in Juárez, had just been sentenced to twenty-four years. "You're doing us a wrong!" he shouted. "Suly Ponce! You're corrupt! You bow down to Chito Solís. Come on, Suly Ponce!" the prisoner hollered. "I respect the authorities, but you're doing this citizen wrong, accusing us falsely, every one of us!"

Rosales Juárez and the other prisoners were the presumed members of the gang known as Los Rebeldes (the Rebels),

---

* In Mexican courts, prisoners testify within a barred cell inside the courtroom.

detained since 1996 as the suspected perpetrators of various femicide murders whose victims had been discovered in brownfield lots on the outskirts of Juárez, including the sub-divisions Lote Bravo and Lomas de Poleo. Together with the other defendants, including Abdel Latif Sharif, alias El Egipcio, and a member of the gang known as Los Toltecas, the men were some of the few suspects arrested for the femicides and were finally facing their day in court. Los Rebeldes had by that time festered eight years in prison without receiving a charge. They were initially detained after the Juárez police, headed by Arturo Chávez Chávez, argued that these men had received orders to commit the murders from El Egipcio, who was detained in 1995, two years after the bodies of murdered women started hitting the streets throughout the borderlands. The version that the state prosecutor told in court was that, in order to throw investigators off his scent, from his prison cell Sharif ordered the men to continue killing women. As proof against the suspects, however, the prosecutor had no evidence besides confessions. Furthermore, only one of those confessions, which implicated an inmate who was later forced to testify against others, was taken without "irregularities."

The sentencing of the suspected murderers, postponed for nearly a decade, took place in the first days of 2005 and was the result of the recent change in policy giving more power to the executive branch, which oversees the attorney general and state prosecutor offices and has de facto control over the legislative and judicial branches. One of the first political resolutions of newly elected Chihuahuan governor José Reyes Baeza was to resolve a number of high-impact criminal cases, focusing on the femicides of the past ten years. Trying to actually solve these cases did little but expose the sad state of the penal system. The international media at the time was reporting that almost every criminal investigation in Chihuahua was riddled with inconsistencies. One of the sharpest criticisms against the justice system came from a UN-sponsored investigation of the charges against Los Rebeldes, including El Egipcio, Gustavo González Meza and Víctor García Uribe (known respectively as La Foca [the Seal] and El Cerillo [the Match]), who were the suspected murderers of eight women discovered dead in a cotton field in 2001. Presented in November of 2003, the UN report was damning. In Chihuahua, the report claimed, the judicial branch has no autonomy, something that should be at the core of delivering justice and due process. Particularly troubling, Juárez judges favored the eyewitness testimony of police officers, especially in high-impact cases, leading to grave violations of impartiality. All allegations made in the femicide cases, the report went on to claim, lacked scientific proof and were a result of confessions made under torture. Gaps in due process were part of a larger pattern, and state judges should have ordered them investigated, recognizing them as the human rights violations that they were. The essential first step, the report concluded, especially in a country "where arbitrary detention and torture are consistently documented as common practices among police forces," would be the unequivocal rejection of all evidence suspected to have been wrongly obtained.

The morning of the trial, the six Rebel inmates were taken out of their cells, led down a long hallway to the prison doors, down an exterior walkway outside the prison walls, and then, still not knowing where they were being taken, led into the courtroom. After eight years in lock-up, they would finally hear their sentencing for the deaths of six victims, two of whom had never been identified. Along with their time in prison, they'd be fined between 20,000 and 27,000 pesos ($1,500 to $2,100) for each victim, a figure based on the annual salary of each woman killed. The defendants, despite the seriousness of the charges, had, for all practical purposes, zero legal representation that day. Only one of them, the only one to be exonerated, had previously met with a lawyer. The other five met their public defenders for the first time that morning, after they'd been tried. Given the irregularities of how their cases were handled, each of the newly condemned men, after receiving their sentence and before being issued out of the courtroom, pleaded their innocence to the cameras. Rosales was the most insistent, yelling that even the witnesses were illegally detained and later tortured by the state police in order to testify against him. The other men told reporters that the police officials who had detained and interrogated them had recently been added to a known list of negligent government employees who had filed contradictory reports. Rosales added that they hadn't even been allowed to defend themselves. He had communicated with a lawyer at one point over the years, but the contact had been cut off after police officers threatened the lawyer. "They [the policemen] told him [the lawyer]," Rosales described, "'you want to get the same specialty treatment as Mario Escobedo?'" Escobedo, who had defended the Seal and the Match in court, was assassinated in 2002. Before being dragged out from the courtroom holding cell, Rosales called out: "Justice for the women of Chihuahua. Don't let injustice and impunity prevail."

The judge presiding over the case of Los Rebeldes was Javier Pineda Arzola, husband of the recently named State Attorney General Patricia González, who, in a recent saga of high-profile condemnations and exonerations, had freed the famous singer Gloria Trevi after five years in prison for the kidnapping, corruption and abuse of young girls.

A second ring of supposed serial femicide murderers, Los Toltecas, was sentenced just a few minutes after Los Rebeldes, on the same day, January 6, 2005, in the Fourth Sentencing Court, only a few yards down the hall. The four prisoners listened to their sentencing in the same fashion, behind courtroom bars. In 1999, they were accused of the murders of six women in Juárez, though the only piece of evidence presented against them was the confession of a fellow gang member, Jesús Manuel Guardado Márquez, alias El Tolteca, obtained after hours of torture at the hands of state police officers. Guardado Márquez was the only one of the suspected murderers who was identified by a victim (a young woman he had mistakenly thought dead). He would be sentenced to sixty-three years in prison for the murders of five other women, two of whom were never identified and whose bodies were so disfigured it would have been nearly impossible to tell how they had been killed. It didn't matter. El Tolteca was probably the only one of the prisoners that most people in Juárez considered to be, if not a serial killer, then at least criminally abusive. A young woman had testified that on the night of March 19, 1999, while riding alone on the maquila bus, El Tolteca, who was the driver, had pulled over, attempted to rape her, beat her and then left her on the side of the road for dead. When I interviewed him, Guardado denied the accusation, arguing that when he had confessed to leaving her "asleep" on the side of the road, it was because the police had forced him to do so. As for the other murders, there was no evidence presented against him in court. Guardado was sentenced to sixty-three years in prison, the maximum sentence a convicted femicide murderer had received thus far in the state.

Guardado is a Juárez native who went to school through only the sixth grade. In 2005, he was thirty-two years old and the father of two daughters and one son, who, after he was detained, spent the following six years plus being shuttled from children's shelter to children's shelter. Guardado didn't know his lawyer, who was, as in the cases of Los Rebeldes, assigned to him only on the day of his trial. Thin and dark-skinned, he was barely five feet tall, and on the day of his sentencing he wore a red sweater with a hole in one of the shoulders. In 2009, when the murder rate was soaring throughout the city, both of his daughters, by then teenagers, would be found horrifically murdered, their bodies showing signs of being tortured and dragged along the ground; one of them was found without an eye. An administrator at one of the shelters where the girls had been raised told me, as I was writing an article on their murders, that she always believed that their father was innocent, that the guilty one was their mother, who had been bribed to hand him over to the authorities and subsequently dumped her son and two daughters at the door of their paternal grandmother. El Tolteca would see his daughters (aged seventeen and eighteen) for the last time on one of the outdoor patios of the Cereso prison, lying inside their coffins.

Just days after the sentencing of Los Rebeldes and Los Toltecas on January 6, 2005, inmate José Luis Rosales Juárez surprised the media by calling a press conference inside the prison. He had been continuing to fight his charges and wanted to present his proof. Tall, thin and only twenty-eight years old, the prisoner slicked back his curly hair and tucked a dress shirt into his beige prison pants before appearing in front of reporters. Walking into the receiving room, where the press was already waiting, with a yellow envelope and a copy of the Mexican Constitution under his arm, he was alone, without any legal representation. He also carried a copy of the penal code and a list of the irregularities and instances of negligence in his treatment at the prison. In an anxious, rapid speech, Rosales Juárez told the press that in 1996 he was detained, without an arrest warrant, and then beaten. The prisoner had only studied through the fifth grade, but he valiantly defended himself and read his papers at full speed while citing numerous precedents and various legal terms. He repeatedly told reporters that he "worked on cars." When I asked him why he hadn't asked his public defender to present all the facts at his trial, he responded that he barely remembered the name of his lawyer and that the few times he had spoken with him, the lawyer had openly admitted that he didn't know much about his case. "Look into this for yourselves," Rosales told his audience. "Look into Suly Ponce Prieto [lead prosecutor in the femicide cases] and the circumstances of his investigation and who ordered him to arrest me, self-defender 328/97, who should be set free according to articles 14, 16 and 20 of the constitution." At the end of his presentation he said that it was upon reading the constitution that he realized for the first time that even public officials could be detained and processed for committing abuses against citizens. He spoke as if struck by epiphany: "This is the injustice that I'm suffering, but I have faith in God."

Shortly after Rosales's trial, I met with Abdel Latif Sharif, alias El Egipcio, imprisoned for the murder of seventeen-year-old Elizabeth Castro. Like the others, Sharif found himself in a Chihuahuan prison fighting to prove his innocence. He wore his hair closely cropped and brushed straight down. He had been a chemist before his imprisonment, and in prison he learned to speak fluent Spanish. His case was a tangle of aberrations, beginning with the fact that the prosecutor presented the court with victim remains that did not match the characteristics—in skin color or stature—of the missing person El Egipcio was charged with murdering. Only two testimonies held up in court: two waiters, who worked at a downtown Juárez bar, Joe's Place, had seen Sharif and the girl walk out of the bar together. Castro had disappeared in August of 1995, and five days after the family initially filed the missing person report, the police found a body, in advanced stages of decomposition, left abandoned in an arroyo. Without a shred of evidence, they claimed the body they had found was Castro's. Sharif was detained in October of the same year as the presumed murderer but wouldn't be sentenced until eight years later, when the state ordered the apprehension of another half a dozen persons for committing crimes of femicide. Sharif's sentencing, having received great international attention, was reviewed by the UN, which put out a report delineating how his case fit the pattern of accusations and confessions made under torture.

Rampant corruption aside, the lack of professionalism in police investigations was so pitiful throughout the 1990s that dozens of femicide criminal investigation reports were lacking such basic information as where the bodies had been found. Yet another international body examining the investigations was the Argentine Team of Forensic Anthropologists, who at the beginning of 2005 reported that every case they came across was fraught with wrongdoings and that half of the victims' bodies would have to be re-identified in order to begin to clean up the system. The Argentine team underlined the obvious, that one of the major obstacles in reopening the cases and issuing justice was the manner in which the bodies had been exhumed: at least thirty victims had been buried in a mass grave, each placed in a plastic bag without a sign or tag to later re-identify them. It was even possible, the forensic team described, that some of the bags had torn, with remains from various victims mixing together in the common grave. Their report claimed that in many cases Mexican investigators failed to follow the most basic clues to help identify the victims. One example they cited described a victim murdered in 1994 who wore a ring with a series of initials and the inscription "Hidalgo Business Academy, GEN II, 1987." The unidentified body was buried a month after it was found, and it took ten years for an investigator to call the Hidalgo Academy to inquire about students who had attended the school in 1987.

With public prosecutors' glaring negligence in the femicide investigations, international pressure forced the hand of the federal government to create a special body to investigate, shed light on and bring justice to the mounting cases: on January 30, 2004, the government created a special commission to the prosecutor's office to investigate crimes against women in Juárez. Soon after its creation, however, under the Vicente Fox administration, the new team determined that many cases were so full of inconsistencies that they would forever remain "impossible to resolve."

The federal prosecutor's office, run by lawyer María López Urbina, concluded that the state investigations, especially those begun in the early 1990s, lacked the basic "elements that would allow for further advancements." In reviewing the records, López Urbina concluded that investigators commonly committed negligent errors such as failing to take testimony from the persons who had discovered the bodies.

Not all was lost, however, for the federal government. In order to "fight impunity," a list was made in July 2004 of eighty-one state prosecutor officials who had omitted facts from various cases and were thus effectively responsible for impeding justice for the victims and their families. Unfortunately, the plan was short-sighted and short-lived, for the responsibility to indict the listed state prosecutor officials fell on the shoulders of the state prosecutor's office itself, which would go on to determine that only five of the eighty-one officers would face prison time. Among those five was Suly Ponce, who Rosales Juárez bitterly complained about during his press conference. According to the public prosecutor's office, the remaining seventy-six officers were negligent because of a simple lack of preparation or proper resources to adequately complete their jobs. In the end, it was these exonerated officers who presented evidence against and prosecuted El Egipcio, Los Rebeldes and Los Toltecas.

In the series of trials triggered by the change of government in Chihuahua, not all of the accused femicide murderers were found guilty. A husband and wife, Ulises Perzával and Cynthia Kiecker, both artisans and latter-day hippies, were detained in Chihuahua City in May of 2003 and accused of the murder of a young woman whose body was found weeks earlier. They were charged (and later found innocent) for the murder of Viviana Rayas, who had disappeared from Chihuahua in March of the same year. The couple's lawyers fought for the next year and a half, arguing that the accusation was based solely on a confession taken from two witnesses under torture. But what ultimately saved Kiecker was her American citizenship: the US government pressured Mexico for her release. Her family was also fortunate enough to have on-hand resources to pay over $180,000 to the lawyers who successfully convinced the court that the confessions were illegally obtained and the investigation riddled with grave errors. The couple was finally exonerated in 2004 and immediately left Mexico.

The methods of interrogation used in the Kiecker and Perzával case seem cut out from archives of Mexico's 1970s dirty war. In plain sight, a group of men in civilian clothing poured out of a white truck on the afternoon of May 31, 2003, and *levantaron,* literally "lifted" or kidnapped, one of the witnesses from downtown Chihuahua, where he worked selling street sketches. The kidnappers were state police officers who, insulting the man, forced him into their truck and took him to the Chihuahua Police Academy.

"That was where they tortured me with a bath towel," the victim, who didn't want to reveal his name, described to me. "They tried to strangle me, and they were asking me if I knew Ulises and I told them that I did. Then they asked me if I knew Viviana and I told them that I didn't. They showed me a photo of the lady and I told them, 'I don't know her.'"

The policemen told "the witness" that he needed to testify that Ulises and Cynthia had killed Viviana. "They told me about some party. The officer yelled at me: 'Look, don't be an idiot, don't you want to tell the truth?' And I told him, 'What truth?' because I didn't know what he was talking about, and he told me, 'Wasn't it true that he beat her with a club?' I said to him, 'I don't know,' and then they tortured me again. They sprayed me with water and shocked me with wires on my back and in my private parts. I got scared and I told them yes, yes, they did it with a club." He added that he met Cynthia on the same day of his "confession," in the bunkroom of the police academy. A young red-haired woman, Cynthia was crying and told him that she didn't know what was going on, that they had come to her house late the night before and broken down the door, dragged her almost an entire block away and then pushed her into a truck and put a bag over her head. The man would meet other witnesses later that night in the bunkroom. They were all handcuffed to their beds. The next day, they pulled Cynthia out of the room, and a few minutes later she came back crazed and crying: she had seen Ulises, who was beaten and had a swollen knee and black burn marks on his stomach. The sound of electricity sparking against wet human flesh would fill the bunkroom for hours. It was a sound, "the witness" said in his statement, that he would never forget.

But torture wasn't the only violation of justice in the case. The couple's lawyers were able to prove inconsistencies in the way investigators had found and identified the body and later located the couple they claimed was responsible for the murder. For example, a day before they identified the victim, a police officer had already reported that Ulises Perzával was under investigation for the victim's murder. These irregularities were a forecast of the many cases to come against presumed femicide culprits. But few defendants had the resources Cynthia Kiecker used to defend herself. One of the couple's lawyers, Miguel Zapién, told me that what stands between liberty and jail for someone in Mexico is, very simply, money. Most femicide defendants were fighting "state emergency charges," he explained, with the entire state apparatus against them. "If

[Cynthia] hadn't been American," Zapién explained, "she'd still be in jail. It's rare that a Mexican would have the money she had to defend herself." Nearly half of the prisoners in the state of Chihuahua relied on public defenders. In Juárez that year, there were ten public defenders who handled about 3,000 cases for a variety of crimes. That's 300 clients for each public defender.

The exoneration of Kiecker and Perzával was an act of justice, but it wasn't any comfort to the family of the victim, left as they were without any explanation as to what had happened to their daughter and knowing that her killer was free. Cirilo Rayas, Viviana's father, headed a government office and was able to put a little pressure on the state. "But if Kiecker and Perzával aren't the murderers, then someone made a big mistake, and that someone is the public prosecutor's office. They were the ones accusing the couple of doing it," Rayas told me one cold morning in December 2004 in an interview conducted at a downtown cafeteria. He said that he felt swindled in every direction. Not even the DNA identification of the body, he claimed, was reliable.

Nearly everybody I've met who has come in contact with the Chihuahua criminal system over the femicide cases has described it as the worst experience of their lives: the victims don't get justice, the defendants lack basic guarantees of safety or legal proofs against them—which makes it highly probable that the actual killers remain at large—and our entire state is left in the dark.

I got a close look into this dark swamp of injustice between November 2004 and March 2005, when I was assigned the justice beat for *El Diario*, the daily newspaper of Chihuahua City, which rests two hundred miles south of the border.

While the presumed femicide culprits were being sentenced, officials in the state capital were taking initial steps to convert the justice system from the method of written testimony—as Los Rebeldes and Los Toltecas were tried—to the method of oral testimony (similar to the court proceedings seen in the United States), which would presume innocence until proven guilty and, supposedly, put an end to confessions taken under torture. Covering both the cases and the reforms kept me frequently inside the prisons, the courts, and the public prosecutor's office, giving me an intimate view of the mudpit of one of the least reputable justice systems in the world.

Near the end of 2004, the lawyer José Chávez Aragón was named chief justice of the Supreme Court of Chihuahua. Dark-skinned, thin, with a mustache, eyeglasses and neatly combed hair, Chávez Aragón had always been a polemic figure within the justice system. Only two years previously, in the position of magistrate, he had exonerated seven Juárez police officers supposedly involved in the murder of Mario Escobedo, the lawyer who was defending the Seal and the Match. Chávez Aragón let the suspects go not because he had proved their innocence but on a technicality. "Their request for an arrest warrant was denied," he excitedly explained during an interview. "And the public prosecutor's office didn't appeal that denial, and if they didn't appeal then whatever they found without the warrant had to be dropped!"

It was the middle of November in 2004 and Chávez Aragón was just settling into his new office in the Supreme Court. He was moving constantly as he spoke to me, archiving folders after scanning their titles or browsing the papers inside, meticulously filing them away in his desk. As he talked he would often raise a hand as if he were giving a speech, emphasizing and enunciating in such a way as to give his words a solemn air. He said, for example, that the police force was the "gua-*ran*-tee" of justice. When I mentioned the inconsistencies that the UN investigation had found in many investigations, he responded that he had barely begun his new position and wasn't yet familiar with the UN report. I told him that the report claimed that Chihuahua's judicial branch suffered a grave lack of independence from the executive branch.

"No," he responded. "As a judge, it's terrible to get orders."

"Why terrible?"

"Well, because I was a judge, and nobody would tell me what to do. No sir!"

"But somebody *tried* to tell you what to do?"

"No, nobody told me what to do. I wouldn't permit it."

"So why do you say it's terrible?"

"Well, I can just imagine ..."

He was playing the part of the classic Mexican politician. As if it were a lighthearted joke he brushed off the idea that police investigators used fall men or engaged in torture to obtain confessions.

He continued: "Why would anybody ever do such a thing? Could you imagine the rule of law we would have? It would be absurd. It would be the jungle. A swamp. Chaos."

"And that's not what this is?"

"No, it's not. I'm sorry, but it's just not. The police force is not what the people think it is; it's not the criminal. The police force guarantees the law; it toils endlessly so that no innocent man is sent to jail and no guilty man stays on the streets."

It wasn't just that officials like Chávez Aragón were so off the mark about the handling of femicide cases, but that these cases, whose investigations were rife with violations, were the only cases that were actually moving forward.

With the guidance of another recently appointed court official, and by reading the literature that was circulating among lawyers about the failures of the justice system, I was able to study various points in the judicial process and use a statistical analysis to catch corruption at various points along the chain of command. The evidence I gathered, based on data provided by the police, the Chihuahua Chief Justice Office, as well as the municipal government of Juárez, showed that the rise in crime was due to the almost complete impunity that reigned in the state: in 2004, only 20 percent of crimes were investigated or, at least, had a file opened; the remaining 80 percent had no official report whatsoever and were swept into what various reporters referred to as the "black list." Of the dwindling pile of the remaining 20 percent open crime investigations, only in slightly more than half of those cases (13 percent in all) had suspects been found through evidence (by 2008, after the full-scale implementation of the judicial reform, the number in which even a single suspect was named would drop to 3 out of 100 crimes), and of those 13 percent of suspects that would eventually go to trial, only one would ever receive a sentence. That translates to a 1 percent conviction rate in Juárez.

Author Guillermo Zepeda Lecuona, from Mexico City's Research Center of Social Development, wrote about the phenomenon of gross impunity in Mexico in his book *Crime Without Punishment*. With only 21 of 100 victims reporting their attacks, Zepeda wrote, Juárez is exactly on par with Kazakhstan and Kyrgyzstan. Add to this that the entire city of Juárez had only ten detectives in charge of investigating violent crimes. In 2004, there were 310 violent deaths—murders or accidental deaths, such as those caused by car accidents—and thousands of other assaults or injuries needing investigation. The city of Chihuahua, by contrast, with a little more than half the population of Juárez and far less crime, had fifteen detectives. The endemic corruption of Juárez—the thirteen policemen formally accused of working with the Juárez Cartel in 2004, or the eighty-one officials reprimanded for their negligence in the investigation of femicides—only exacerbated the high levels of impunity already in effect.

The monstrous corruption and ineptitude of the public prosecutor's office seemed to overshadow the petite woman who had recently been elected to implement an internal overhaul that would address the femicides. In an interview, the ex-judge Patricia González promised to reform the legal system and introduce modern forensic technology to violent crime investigations. Upon taking office, González explained that the judicial crisis of rampant impunity in which Chihuahua, and especially Juárez, found itself was due to administrative disorder and the lack of investigative manuals, not corruption. The problem, she said, was due to a "global" and "decade-long crisis" concerning the mechanisms used to procure justice. The fault of the crisis, in short, was nobody's in particular. "It's not a product of just one factor; it's multifactorial." It was a technical problem. There needed to be more economic resources, more trained experts, laboratories and a more scientifically savvy police force. Chihuahua needed nothing more than incremental improvements to what was already there. "By efficientizing [sic] criminal investigations we will return security and trust to the people. It's not necessary to obtain confessions to prove someone guilty. We can use science and technology, advanced technology. I believe this is a huge step, and, well, history will be the judge."

As long as González remained the primary point of contact for USAID (US Agency for International Development), the US government was more than willing to subsidize her efforts. Meanwhile, USAID was also responsible for funding the state's judicial reform, substituting the written trial system for the oral trial system and enforcing the presumption of innocence. American ambassador Antonio Garza first announced USAID's funding plans in 2005. Thus, after years of being judged by the world as corrupt, incapable and negligent, the Chihuahuan justice system would finally solve all its disastrous problems by the open intervention of the American government.

Drafts of the new compendium of criminal laws in Chihuahua, as well as the many documents explaining the new system, stressed the importance of eliminating the value placed on confessions and eliminating the practice of torture, barring judges from considering confessions made under torture. The burden of proof would fall, as seen on American television, on science and criminology. These fundamental changes, so the legal drafts argued, would work toward transparency, presumed innocence and oral testimony, with the interdependent parts balancing each other and building toward the greater perception of legitimacy, thus allowing the state to resolve its conflicts and maintain social harmony and peace.

USAID subcontracted the organization Proderecho to collect and study available literature on the topic as well as conduct a legal analysis, which they compiled on compact discs and distributed to various lawyers and legislators. The final report included an "analysis of the current justice system in Mexico," followed by a list of the various inadequacies in the national judicial process: that it took place in written form, mostly behind closed doors and with no opportunity for the public to witness proceedings. Proderecho wrote, "the tradition of the written inquisitorial system is so strong that proceedings unfold while officials are focused on writing documents that decide the outcome of each case, leaving the defendants in the dark, with little understanding of their case, and without any trust in the legal process." Judges rarely saw the defendants, the witnesses testifying against them or the experts involved in the case. Proderecho's long report went on to state that the American-style adversarial process hinges on the burden of proof and the presumption of innocence, implying that suspects remain free if the police have no evidence against them. The inquisitorial process, which was still in use throughout Mexico, including in the state of Chihuahua, was a legacy of monarchical governments that no longer existed and was created to protect the state rather than the individual. The old system considered confession to be the ultimate burden of proof.

The judicial world of the state capital was thus going through a revolutionary upheaval. In parliament, where Chávez Aragón had assured me that nobody was being tortured in Chihuahua, there were various conferences with international experts, mostly from Spain, who spoke openly about the archaic state penal system. For hours the presenters talked about the importance of justice in a healthy democracy. One doctor of law from the University of Salamanca, Nieves Sanz, drew signs of disapproval from the likes of Chávez Aragón when she vigorously pointed out that the articles of crimes listed in the inquisitorial penal code of Chihuahua began by condemning crimes committed against "the security of the state," such as rebellion, while murder wasn't listed until eighty-seven articles later. The law, she argued, prioritized not the protection of life but the survival of the state. A democracy should begin by defending the well-being of the individual, including the life of the individual, Sanz explained, for which homicide should head the list of crimes that are investigated and penalized.

In the next three years, Chihuahua would become the first Mexican state to apply the new justice system to all crimes. Given the conditions in Juárez and across the state, it seemed well overdue to determine the inquisitorial system archaic. The transition to an adversarial system that respects human rights and hopes to eradicate torture couldn't come any sooner.

However, there was one remaining doubt: in exchange for what was the United States investing so much money in Chihuahua's penal system? The answer was to be found in the documentation of various international organizations like USAID and the World Bank, which were funding judicial reform not only in Chihuahua and throughout Mexico (the complete national reform will go into effect by the end of 2016), but throughout Latin America. The motive for the change wasn't what they had found wrong with the inquisitorial system, and it wasn't the protection of the individual; rather, it was the strengthening of the free market, which had been obstructed by the institutional weaknesses of a slow and archaic justice system. According to the text, "Lessons Learned: Introduction of Oral Process in Latin America," formulated by the Inter-American Development Bank—for which international organizations proposed judicial reforms all across the continent: "the harmful consequences of institutional instability are well-proven and discourage foreign investment —a problem well known to the judiciary. Moreover, economic development invites new subjects into the formal economy of the country, thus creating a demand for new legal services, which, as of now, are impossible to access because they have yet to be incorporated into the justice system."

Repeatedly, the report cites "governability for economic development," which the new penal system would foster. The growth of economies both in the United States and in Latin America, the report continues, are characterized by "more open and competitive forms of transactions," and yet the "institutional weaknesses" of developing countries, particularly the obstacles posed by the archaic penal system, could cause instability and thus increase the cost of operations. In sum, the penal system in places such as Chihuahua presented a potential obstacle for the consolidation of the globalizing economic model. Despite the violence, Juárez would continue to be an important city for American investment and trade. And thus: the United States would attempt to rescue its justice system.

But the implementation of a justice system meant to privilege the market over the individual suffered from a troubled past. One of the participants in the conference, Roberto Bergalli, Argentine professor of sociology of law at the University of Barcelona and director of the International Institute of Juridical Sociology, warned that US participation in judicial reforms in Latin America had a long and negative history. It was exactly these types of interventions, Bergalli explained, that led to the eruption of military groups that staged coups in Brazil, Uruguay, Chile and Argentina. "The impunity and injustice that reigns in these countries is still manifest,"

Bergalli said. "Genocides are still taking place in the streets. Officials who steal public funds remain free. So: I don't see the supposed help or assistance we could hope to receive from these experts or from the investments pouring in to finance more of these same reforms."

I asked Bergalli what he thought specifically about US funds coming into Chihuahua. "I don't know exactly what's happening in Chihuahua," he responded, "or what is going to happen, but I know from experience what happens in Latin America when foreign countries invest in their judicial reforms, or any other type of reform. I know what happened in Guatemala, in El Salvador, in Peru and in Nicaragua. These countries experienced a foreign-led judicial reform, penal reform, trade reform. It may seem natural and comprehensible, but it is unjustifiable that the resources of a rich country pave the roads of a poor country solely so that their businesses may pour in."

The history of the Chihuahuan penal system is full of failures in bringing criminals to justice. Between 2008 and 2010—as statistics would show with the more than 7,000 homicides throughout the city, of which less than 3 percent had open investigations—nobody was able to claim that crimes were punished and individual life was protected. We desperately longed for change. The penal system would need to start functioning if the state wanted to put an end to violence; any other method would merely slow the violence down.

Once again, in February 2005, I came across the definition of impunity that Vicente had shared with me a year earlier. This time it came from Yakin Ertürk, a UN rapporteur of violence against women, who explained: "Impunity is one of the factors that has perpetuated homicides specifically and violence in general. That crimes go unpunished makes it ever easier for those who are committing them." She spoke to me in a brief interview after she had met with Governor José Reyes Baeza and State Attorney General Patricia González at the Governor's Palace of Chihuahua. Ertürk had arrived that same day to learn more of the state's plan to combat femicides in Juárez. "The governor," Ertürk told me, "is putting an emphasis on eradicating impunity, which, I believe, is a good start." As we walked through the halls of the Governor's Palace, she repeated again and again, with each question I asked her, the importance of ending impunity in the state. And when I asked her what she thought was really happening in Juárez, again she responded that given the many reports she had read about the femicides, the central problem was the lack of punishment that left hundreds of crimes unresolved. "I'm trying to understand," she said. "Obviously there are many reports, and one of the principal themes you find in them is the impunity, that the crimes go uninvestigated, that they are not resolved, and that this has exacerbated the problem." As long as impunity is not eradicated, she insisted, all crime, and all violence in general, will become a way of life, making it harder to combat. Boiled down: impunity turns crime into a habit.

7

ARTISTAS ASESINOS

Like Vicente León, El Saik was also detained on May 21, only he was brought in two years earlier, in the spring of 2002, when he was just nineteen years old. A group of state police officers came to his door with an arrest order because, according to crime scene investigators, El Saik had participated in a drive-by shooting that morning targeting a moving car in which Nelson Martínez Moreno, an El Paso native, also nineteen years old, was shot dead. The crime occurred on Vicente Guerrero Street in northern Juárez. El Saik allegedly cut off his victim on Brazil Street and began firing. He hit Nelson in the forehead, another passenger in the left forearm, and barely grazed the back of a third victim. The latter two survived and were able to identify their attacker. They knew where El Saik lived and, wasting no time, went that very day to report the crime to the police. It was only a matter of hours before the police were knocking on El Saik's door.

El Saik was the alias of Éder Ángel Martínez Reyna, a young man who lived on Durango Street in the neighborhood of Bosques de Salvarcar of southeastern Juárez. Ever since he was a boy, El Saik drove his mother crazy by repeatedly running away from home, often for extended periods of time, forcing her to put up missing-person pictures of him around the neighborhood. Growing up in a one-story house, with two-bedrooms crammed into eighty-six square feet, and a common area that served as living room, dining room and kitchen, it seemed inevitable that the boy would spend long hours outside. El Saik did occasionally go to school, but nothing excited him like wandering the streets, where he soon became target and accomplice in various assaults that frequently landed him at the juvenile detention center, the Escuela de Mejoramiento Social para Menores, or the School. His only two passions were art and crime, and for long hours he would sketch the images of his inner world, filling up entire notebooks. When El Saik was growing up in the '90s, there were no recreational areas, parks, libraries, theaters or other public spaces where a kid his age could constructively pass the time or broaden his world. There were only the streets, where, like a factory-made product on an assembly line, thousands of houses as small as his multiplied before him. These tiny houses would often abut vacant lots or maquiladoras, as was the case with El Saik's house, which directly bordered the factory campus Intermex Industrial, where the aquamarine sign of the Siemens Technology Plant still towers over the landscape today. Nearby loom the factories of Motorola, General Electric and Honeywell, among others.

Near Intermex and its neighboring industrial plants on Durango Street and Las Torres Avenue, there are other residential areas, such as the neighborhoods of Horizontes del Sur, Villas de Salvárcar, Torres del Sur, Paseo de las Torres, Valle Dorado, Juárez Nuevo, Las Dunas, Rincón del Sol,

Parajes del Sur, Ampliación Aeropuerto, Morelos I, II, III and IV, and many more. All of them developed around and because of the maquiladoras, though in time they interspersed with shopping malls and older neighborhoods just starting to urbanize, like the neighborhoods of Solidaridad, Los Alcaldes, Zaragoza and Salvárcar. Hundreds of empty lots of various sizes were left in the midst of all the urban boom, creating a patchwork of fragmented islands separated from each other by a sea of dunes and trash that, because of the high crime rate, made for a lethal commute and eliminated any chance of a public space that could generate cohesion or geographic identity: the beautiful desert reduced to an abandoned, filthy landscape, incapable of spurring any feeling of community or belonging.

In an environment so unfit to foster social or communal development, thousands of children and teenagers like El Saik took to the streets, banding together to—at least in the beginning, in the '80s and '90s—talk, skate and break-dance. It was only later that they began fighting over turf, claiming territory with graffiti and dividing themselves into cliques, naming themselves Los Bufones (the Jesters), SWK, CVS, Barrio del Silencio (Barrio of Silence), Los Quinteros and Los Guasones (the Jokers). Whoever tagged their name more than anyone else won control over that quadrant of the neighborhood. The competition was known as "varo," and soon all the main roads were painted in the sometimes beautiful, often illegible and dense calligraphy. It wasn't long before violence became part and parcel of these turf wars. Los Bufones, for example, would use abandoned houses on Jilotepec Avenue, near the high school, Secundaria Técnica 60, as fight clubs where aspiring members—many of them students at the school—earned gang membership by proving their worth in fistfights. These initiations were then switched out with store robberies. By 2000, the teenagers had equipped themselves with firearms. And then came a series of maquiladora robberies and public brawls that for years plagued southeast Juárez, where the city's first neighborhood curfews were imposed in a futile attempt to combat crime. The next plague, a surprise to few, was murder. In only a few years, these once spray-paint-scrawling teenagers of southeastern Juárez made up the majority of the underage delinquents in the city.

Southeast Juárez, which local sociologists termed "New City" or "South City," is where municipal and state officials funneled the housing demands of the maquiladora workers during the economic boom of the mid '80s and '90s, when the city—which supplied more than three of every ten of the nation's industrial jobs—registered a tremendous population increase: more than doubling its inhabitants from less than 600,000 to more than 1,200,000.

The explosive population growth spurred the new Juárenses to use various under-the-table methods to appropriate land. West Juárez, for example, was taken over by a surge of inhabitants who sold their votes in exchange for parcels of land that were virtually inaccessible from greater Juárez, like the foothills of the Sierra de Juárez mountain range, where most roads are still unpaved. Those living in southeast Juárez bought their houses through formal credit loans and were able to access some basic urban services, including paved streets and sidewalks, street lights, potable water and drainage. But like those living in west Juárez, most residents of the southeast also worked for the maquiladoras or in related industries and would never earn more than minimum wage, around 700 pesos a week, or between $60 and $70. And the city didn't bother to equip them with other basic necessary services such as schools, daycares, hospitals and public transportation, which greatly contrasted the treatment that the maquila industry itself enjoyed, including wide and strategically placed roads built to transport their products to international ports of entry. The workers, however, most of them commuting by foot, didn't even have a sidewalk to walk on. The few recreational areas built in their neighborhoods quickly turned into dirty lots, usually empty save for a rusting swing set.

There was a good explanation for the sorry physical and social state of these parts of Juárez. The southeast was urbanized thanks to two former mayors of the Institutional Revolutionary Party, Manuel Quevedo and Jaime Bermudez, who, in December of 1977, decided to invest in the maquila boom—which Bermudez himself played a heavy role in instigating—and bought close to 20,000 acres of land around the airport, practically doubling the size of the city. Quevedo had been mayor only three months, and Bermudez, who would become mayor in 1985, was the new city treasurer. For the two landowners, business took off immediately, and, in the next thirty years, thanks to their economic and political power, they funneled urban growth onto their own properties. They steered public funding set aside for infrastructure—like potable water, drainage, streetlights and roads—toward their own real-estate and construction companies. Their political power enabled them to develop areas that were more and more isolated from the rest of the city, creating the deeply stratified urban sprawl that so characterizes Juárez today. In 2004, for example, Quevedo forced the construction of thousands of housing units on a large estate interchangeably known as

El Barreal or Laguna de Patos, located south of the airport, directly on top of what researchers had warned was a dry riverbed that could easily flood with storm-water run-off from the western sierra. With the summer rains of 2006, thousands of working-class families still paying off their houses were left completely awash for days.

The problems germinating as a result of unregulated development didn't take long to stir up sociologists, journalists and the general citizenry, who spent years arguing not only that the current process of urbanization was corrupt but that spatial isolation was becoming more costly and beginning to hinder city maintenance. This in turn fomented social backwardness, deteriorated and disfigured the landscape, raised the cost and time residents spent on public transportation and, above all, created two extremely disjointed peripheries—the west and the southeast—which created tremendous obstacles for social interaction and was even beginning to divide society at large.

Arguing that it would attract the maquila industry, the government defended the development of the ex-politicians' land even though it put residents farther and farther away from the city center. Urban expansion continued undeterred. By 2000, urbanization was growing at such a rate that 40 percent of Juárez's population, almost 500,000 people in all, moved to those two neighborhoods and their surrounding areas near the factory campuses on Las Torres Avenue, which were divided into low-income subdivisions such as Bosques de Salvarcar, Villas de Salvarcar and Horizontes del Sur.

At the same time, hundreds of children and teenagers were arming themselves and joining the gangs. These were the kids who not long before had merely wanted to tag their names on walls. Now these groups were becoming the deadliest gangs of Juárez. Soon the local authorities attributed four of every ten homicides to gang activity, and in 2002 the members of Los Bufones, Los Quinteros, Barrio del Silencio and others cliques (including El Saik and some of his friends living around the Intermex industrial park) formed a new gang that in only a few years would lead the surge of criminal offenses. They called themselves, so the teenager told the public prosecutor when he was detained, Los Artistas Asesinos. May 21, 2002, marked the first time that reporter Armando Rodríguez printed the name in the Juárez media.

One of the smartest young criminals in the city was credited as having formed Los Artistas Asesinos. Originally from the neighborhood of Morelos II, many remember Jorge Ernesto Sáenz for having been the first gang member to kill a city police officer. Sáenz was known as El Dream. Like El Saik, he came from one of the subdivisions of southeast Juárez and was a talented artist. In fact, before becoming an infamous murderer, he was famous among his neighbors for the quality, detail and vibrant color of his graffiti. He won most of the tagging competitions by scratching his nom de guerre across the neighborhood walls. Tall, thin, with his hair sometimes shaved to the scalp and other times worn long, and almost always carrying a backpack of spray cans, at only sixteen years old El Dream was looked up to by hundreds of neighborhood kids. He used his prestige to recruit other students from Técnica 60 into his clique. As the years went by, his talent as a graffiti artist and his readiness to win turf wars through ever more violent means made him one of the most famous gangsters of his generation. Like El Saik, he was full of potential: smart and physically strong, looking for excitement but tragically surrounded by an environment devoid of any wholesome, or even lawful, stimuli.

Also like El Saik, El Dream committed his first murder at nineteen years old, when he shot to death a maquila security guard in 2001, stealing 279,000 pesos (around $20,000), one of the largest lootings in the history of Juárez. He was caught, arrested and detained at Cereso. El Dream, however, had other ideas. A year into his sentence, in July 2002, he tricked a guard and escaped the prison by using a visitor's name-card that had cost his mother $1,000. She'd bought it from a friend who had visited the prison and had simply claimed he'd lost the name-card when it was time for him to return it at the front desk. Once out on the streets, it didn't take long for El Dream to return to his criminal career. Two weeks after his escape, at about 10 PM on August 7, he and some other gang members from his neighborhood jumped a pair of city policemen guarding a maquiladora in the neighborhood of Jardines del Aeropuerto. The assailants got out of their Cherokee and shot the officers with .40 caliber and 9-millimeter pistols, wounding them both. They took the officers' weapons and radios, dragged them into their car and drove them to a vacant lot in the neighborhood of Hacienda de las Torres. One of the officers, suffering from three gunshot wounds, compliantly slumped over when he was violently shoved out of the car, but his partner, thirty-two-year-old Ubaldo Cruz Gonzales wanted to save himself and started to run away. El Dream shot him in the back and, standing over him, fired again into the back of his head. The group of young gang members then squealed away in their Cherokee only to abandon it some miles ahead in the subdivision Praderas del Sur, where they stole a van from a young woman at gunpoint and, continuing their madcap escape, crashed it into a street post on Tomas Fernandez Avenue. Moments later, they stole another van from two other young women. El Dream was driving when the city police finally caught up to them on Tecnológico Avenue. That night El Dream stole a total of three vehicles at gunpoint, wounded a transit cop and killed a Juárez city police officer. He was barely twenty years old.

In 2002, back at Cereso, El Dream and El Saik became closer, spending months planning their next escape, drawing intricate maps that would later be confiscated and leaked to the media. There was tremendous tension in the prison, where 3,500 inmates lived in a space made for less than 2,000 and cells were filled to twice their capacity. Many had to sleep on top of blankets laid out on the concrete floors. The air conditioning was always set too low in the summer, and the heater barely worked in the winter. Cockroaches made their homes even in the inmates' food. El Saik and El Dream felt that they were going insane locked away in their tiny cells.

In April of 2003, it was El Saik who provoked a state of emergency in the prison when he and three other inmates—all of whom were identified as friends of El Dream—kidnapped a guard, took over one of the watchtowers and procured three rifles, a revolver and a grenade launcher. Setting their plan in motion took little more than a cup of shrimp. El Dream offered the snack to a guard who was watching a group of inmates play a game of softball, and when the guard reached for the spiced shrimp through the barred fence dividing the prison sports area, an inmate grabbed the guard by his feet and another threatened him with a makeshift weapon. El Saik and his accomplices took over a watchtower and the weapons inside it, mobilizing 200 city and state police officers, who managed to force the inmates into dropping their arms in less than twenty minutes. Despite the excitement, El Saik wasn't satisfied. A few days later, in May 2003, he tried to escape again, only this time through the air-conditioning ducts in his cell. He managed to climb up to a rooftop before he was caught, only a few yards away from the barbwire fence that separated him from the prison parking lot. Again, hundreds of public officers surrounded him. After this final attempt, his prison conditions became far more severe. He could no longer leave his cell and was locked away in solitary confinement.

The Cereso prison cells are almost all the same, with an area measuring three yards by three yards and cement beds that jut out of the walls with thin mats as cushioning. The inmates are responsible for procuring all toiletries. Most of the cells face either an open-air corridor or the central patio, which is outfitted with kiosks where inmates sell goods to each other, from candy to lunches and juices to old Foosball tables. Before the inmates were separated by gang affiliation, these lodgings served to divide them according to the nature of their crime.

In spring 2004, a special unit was built for those the prison considered its most dangerous inmates, including El Saik and El Dream. This unit, called Ward 16, stood in contrast with the rest of Cereso in that it was a windowless polygon. It was built on the northeastern side of the prison, just a few yards from the outworn courts of the old penal system. Inside, the cells and hallways of Ward 16 were even smaller than in the rest of the prison, and the central patio offered no recreational space or even a view to the outside world. The internment plan for the unit called for twenty-two hours of cell-time and an allotment of only two hours to walk around the enclosed patio, with each inmate given patio-time by himself. The only human contact these inmates, all of whom were under constant supervision, would have was with the criminology and psychology staff.

In his isolation, El Saik found reprieve by returning to drawing. A few months in, he was able to start taking classes in oil painting; soon he began selling his works to other prisoners who paid with money earned by giving each other tattoos. Over the years, the hobby turned out to have its benefits. In 2006, four years after becoming the first registered Artista Asesino in Juárez, El Saik won first place in a national prisoner painting contest.

Other young men like El Dream and El Saik, most of them either from southeast Juárez or funneled from the School, were starting to fill out the cells in Cereso's Ward 16. It was a new breed of murderer, Juárenses of twenty or younger, among whom Vicente León—arriving to Ward 16 on May 23, 2004, after being charged with the murder of his parents and sister—fit right in. As nobody presented his birth certificate, he spent his first twelve days of incarceration in the adult Cereso prison. Uziel, meanwhile, was sent straight to Ward 7 of the adult prison, where Los Aztecas and any Christian inmates were confined. The prison authorities, dealing with ever more explosive episodes of violence, alleged that the old friends were separated to avoid a possible confrontation.

It was during his brief initial stay in Cereso when criminologists interviewed Vicente for the first time, qualifying that his murders were committed not with "endogenous" or internal motives but with "exogenous" motives. In his record, the experts noted that they were dealing with an "intelligent, high-risk delinquent" who came from a highly violent urban zone. A separate psychological evaluation done by prison psychologists indicated that Vicente's negative attitude and his antisocial conduct were due to a dangerous mix of low frustration tolerance, a tendency to become agitated, impulsive behavior, poor judgment skills, a marked resistance to authority, and a childhood spent in a highly criminogenic environment. The chief of the Cereso prison's Department of Criminology warned that these characteristics were seen more and more frequently in the local criminal youth in the prison, as in the cases of El Dream and El Saik.

Vicente finished his first stay in Ward 16 on June 4, 2004, when the Second Court received his birth certificate and authorized his transfer to the School of Social Improvement for Minors. There, teenagers from southeast Juárez made up the majority of the population. In 2004, authorities estimated that there were around 300 gangs in Juárez fighting for control of the streets, the majority of them coming from the southeast, where Los Artistas Asesinos were already the undisputed rulers. Like El Dream, these new gang members had veered away from the classic gangster dress code influenced by the cholo-style of western Juárez: baggy pants and shaved heads. Instead, the kids from the southeast chose a more modern and "neater" style. They snubbed sagging pants and opted for stylized jags and bolts shaved into their eyebrows and sideburns. Police identified them by their tattoos: the intertwined letters ASA, the number 2 on one arm and the letter A on the other ("Double A," for Los Artistas Asesinos), or the full gang name spelled out on each arm. Not infrequently, the tattoo calligraphy was inspired by the hip-hop group Cypress Hill, whose Latino-influenced music was an inspiration for the young gangsters:

I'm just another local
Kid from the street getting paid for my vocals
Here is something you can't understand
How I could just kill a man.

Murders committed by adolescents were becoming ever more frequent in Juárez. A statistic published in 2004, after Vicente's parricide, indicated that, since 1999, there had been 176 minors detained under suspicion of murder: one teen arrested for murder every ten days over the course of five years. Despite the numbers, Vicente was treated as if he were an extraordinary case in the School. Even in this violent border city, a sixteen-year-old parricide seemed extreme. The School's administration noted the manipulative influence Vicente held over his accomplices, and to circumvent the risk factor they decided to confine the minor to an isolated cell. They also submitted him to almost constant psychological assessment and treatment, placed him under observation and only let him leave his cell to go to the washroom or eating hall. Thus, Vicente spent the first two and a half months of his five-year term nearly completely isolated from fellow inmates.

At the time, the School of Social Improvement for Minors was located in an old building on Norzagaray Boulevard, right on the bank of the Rio Grande in the heart of downtown Juárez. Just as on the lonely tract of land on Zaragoza Road where Vicente dumped and torched the bodies of his parents and younger sister, the only thing he could see from his cell at night were the amber lights of the border-wall infrastructure between Mexico and the United States. It was there where, according to the official file, he suffered the first of his many bouts of insomnia. The prison psychologists warned from the beginning that Vicente, instead of showing signs of remorse, demonstrated the opposite: in his complex criminal mind he thought that his parricide made the other inmates look up to him.

On his sleepless nights in the small cell overlooking the Rio Grande, it wasn't remembering his murder that kept him awake. He didn't feel bad about what he had done. He didn't even lament being locked up or seeing his criminal talent go to waste. Nor did he miss his parents or sister. He missed, slightly, little C.E., the only member of his family who he considered worthy to be alive. Aside from C.E. there wasn't a human being that provoked any feeling, any respect or affection, any sentiment of authority or even fear. Nothing. Inside his sixteen-year-old body there was a feeling of emptiness. He was, as the psychologists determined, "incapable of establishing positive interpersonal relationships" with other human beings. This emptiness soon morphed into severe insomnia, which then lead to a deep depression that lasted through the end of 2004. The pale skin around his eyes started to darken, his face tightening over his bones as he lost weight. He continued to spend the majority of his days in isolation, receiving no visitors. Nor did he express any emotion before prison officials. He would never again in his life agree to another interview with the press, and he refused to see two of his uncles, the only family members who ever tried to visit him.

By the beginning of 2005 Vicente's rehabilitation plan required him to take classes, beginning with the first quarter of high school of the detention center's education program. In class for the first time since the day after committing the crime, he saw Eduardo, his old friend, who had also passed through a dark period at the detention center, although in a manner quite different from Vicente. Eduardo suffered from deep feelings of remorse and guilt for what he had done in the house on Rosita Road, as well as for having failed his parents. Their forgiveness, however, would become a great driving factor in overcoming his depression, which, according to subsequent diagnoses, he ultimately achieved. Still, he was aggrieved by the idea of having caused his family such pain, especially as he began to understand the continuing toll of his actions; his brother, for one, had had to change schools. One of the key differences between the two young murderers was the amount of family support each received: while Vicente wouldn't see a single member of his family, Eduardo went to therapy every Saturday with his parents. He began to shine as a student. He even graduated from high school and was given the freedom to leave the School to take classes at the Juárez Institute of Technology. He also received visits not just from family members but from past girlfriends who would accompany him to evening dances held at the School. At one point in his sentence, he joined a band and even won a singing contest.

Vicente, meanwhile, was developing a sort of stage fright borne out of what the prison psychologists termed "media overexposure," which became an obstacle in his basic social rehabilitation. The most common activities, those that Eduardo was easily accomplishing, became terrifying for Vicente. He didn't see himself the way the city saw him; it was hard for him to believe that a place so full of impunity could judge him as the most brutal of its criminals.

Soon, the routine at the detention center, however much it bored him, started to help. Even having to wake up at six in the morning when the guards came and knocked on all the cell doors made the days seem less of a struggle. He hardly had time to think about the tedium of being alive. Like all the other inmates, Vicente went straight to the showers after wake-up call; from there, he returned to clean his room and then went to the mess hall for breakfast; he went to classes, and in the afternoons he attended a workshop in either carpentry, mechanics, ironwork or computer skills. Vicente preferred carpentry, spending his afternoons making chairs, tables, bookcases and shelves or repairing home furniture that people from the neighborhood would bring for the inmates to fix. Obligatory sports participation took up even more of his day and his energy. He still regularly attended therapy. With all of his schoolwork, the workshops, the therapy and the increasingly consistent contact with other inmates, he slowly began to come out of himself. Even the spring desert sun played a part in Vicente's healing. By May of 2005, completing the first year of his sentence, he had almost completely shaken off his depression. He started offering to wash the guards' cars to earn a little money so he could buy clothes and notebooks, as he was one of the few inmates who wasn't helped by his family, meaning that all of his basic living necessities were covered by the School's social work department. This didn't seem to bother him. Despite being under constant scrutiny and oversight, without even realizing it, Vicente soon started feeling like he fit in; although he was the only parricide, there were dozens of other convicted murderers in the School. With them, Vicente shared not only a capacity for brutality but a marked intolerance for anything that got in the way of his desires. Some of these inmates were starting to call themselves Artistas Asesinos, and with them, once again feeling his penchant for leadership,

Vicente celebrated his eighteenth birthday on October 27, 2005.

Unlike Eduardo, who due to his good conduct was able to remain at the School after he had turned eighteen, Vicente aged out. His maternal grandparents, aunts and uncles all agreed with the School's prognosis on the unlikelihood of his social rehabilitation and petitioned that he be transferred to the adult prison as soon as possible. Vicente's relatives said that they would feel safer if the murderer raised among them was locked up in Cereso prison, and the directors of the School complied, ordering his transfer by the end of 2005.

Vicente wasn't surprised by the news. Not at all. He knew why Eduardo was able to stay at the School, and why he didn't get the same treatment. After a drive of just over ten miles, just as afternoon started its dip into evening, at 3:59 PM, he arrived at the Juárez Municipal Police Office at Cereso on November 9, 2005. He was immediately submitted to a medical exam that determined him to be a healthy eighteen-year-old man, six feet tall, 160 pounds and free of neurological disorders. He was determined to be a "primary delinquent" showing signs of being highly aggressive and with a low possibility for rehabilitation. Two photographs, a headshot and a profile, were printed on the upper right-hand side of his case file. In the photo, his brown eyes stared blankly at the camera. His adolescent features contrasted with his summary description: "Inmate with high criminal capacity and of maximum danger." The conditions in the prison were already so tense by the end of 2005 that inmates weren't divided according to type of crime, as they had been just a year previously, but according to gang affiliation. All prisoner files indicated the "criminal association," which either the inmate would claim himself or would be identified by prison officials; the options were "Aztecas" or "Mexicles." Vicente admitted his own affiliation: Artista Asesino. After the intake interview, Vicente was led into the ward where he would spend the third of the four phases of his imprisonment: Ward 16.

8

LOS AZTECAS

There was a roar in the distance. The floor started to shake. Two hundred members of the Los Mexicles gang stood in their tiny cells in Ward 4, listening to the growing thunder of a stampede coming toward them. More than 1,000 Aztecas were seconds away from crossing the last of the dividing hallways of Cereso prison, separating them from their sworn enemies. Los Mexicles were at a major disadvantage. They were in lockdown after having protested on the prison rooftop for having their visitation hour revoked. The morning before, one of the Mexicle prisoners was found nearly dead, having been stabbed more than seventy times. The fear was everywhere, and increasing. The tension that had built for years finally exploded on the cold morning of December 17, 2005. At around 11 AM, someone opened a prison door and hundreds of angry Azteca "soldiers," armed with sticks, cudgels, bats and iron rods, poured into the patio, the hallways and the cells, beating any Mexicle in sight. Some of the Aztecas were even wearing helmets and carried crowd-control shields that they took from the prison storeroom. In the twenty-five years of the overcrowded Juárez prison system, the following minutes were the bloodiest on record. The police and prison guards failed to intervene for two hours, and Los Aztecas were able to wound forty Mexicles and murder six. They killed one Mexicle with fourteen stab-wounds in the chest; another had forty-nine wounds in his neck and chest; another, whose skull was crushed, suffered sixty stab wounds to his body. Many of the Mexicles who were able to save themselves did so by locking themselves in their cells, stacking their concrete-slab beds against the doors. On the other side of the prison, the Aztecas, still searching for victims, smashed glass and broke down doors, trying to gain access to Ward 1 and Ward 3, where there were stray Mexicles waiting to be found.

Armando Rodríguez wrote about what he saw of the prison brawl from where he was stationed, just outside the security door. Upon arrival, he witnessed paramedics running out of the prison with the day's first patient. They placed the victim on a gurney and put an oxygen mask over his face. Then they cut off his shirt and pants, revealing multiple knife wounds in the chest, abdomen and legs. The victim also had a wound on his forehead and his face was covered in blood. The paramedics tried to resuscitate him, compressing his chest, but they couldn't bring him back. On this bloodiest day in the history of Cereso, the first victim was abandoned almost as soon as he died. With limited resources and the onslaught of wounded inmates, the medics had to free up the gurney for the next victim, ditching the prisoner's body against a wall. He was laid out on the ground, face up, his pants around his legs and the blood from his wounds still seeping out into the dirt. A few minutes later the medics came out with a new body. Like a production line, four more bodies would quickly be lined up next to the first.

That day, newspapers reporting on the brawl mentioned a fact that underlined the barbarity of Juárez's prisons: all the firsthand testimonies, as well as the accounts of the relatives who spoke with the prisoners, claimed that it was the prison guards themselves who opened the doors for Los Aztecas, even arming them with weapons, helmets and shields. It was thus a brawl that was not only permitted but even initiated by the prison authorities working under the current mayor, Héctor Murguía, who only four months before had launched the plan "Clean Cereso," promising to rid the prison of drugs but instead working to isolate and weaken the members of the previously dominant gang, Los Mexicles, leaving Los Aztecas—who would become the armed division of the Vicente Carrillo Cartel—in complete control of the prison. As one of the most important drug distribution centers of the city, Cereso was also one of the most stable markets—more than 1,000 addicts were locked inside—operating under a system of corruption that nobody made an effort to hide.

Although top officials were never under scrutiny, the investigations of the December 17 prison brawl found that at least thirteen guards, a sergeant, as well as a top prison warden were guilty of "instigating" Los Aztecas, opening their cell doors and giving them arms and protective gear. An article in the December 30 edition of *El Diario* reported that a possible motive for the prison warden, the head of security, as well as for Los Aztecas themselves, was a rearrangement of power in order to expand the drug market. The participation of the various levels of authority in drug trafficking had no limits in Juárez, and Cereso wasn't an exception. Under the control of

Murguía, from the last days of 2005 until the middle of 2007, Cereso turned into a bloodbath: in a year and a half there were seventeen murders, all victims killed by members of Los Aztecas and all under the close watch of prison officials.

Both inside and outside of prison, Los Aztecas had worked for the Juárez Cartel since the early 2000s. They were one of the organization's key armed wings, ferrying drugs across the border by car, guarding houses in northeast El Paso and distributing merchandise across US highways to various city hubs, including Atlanta, Dallas, Chicago and Denver. And when members of La Línea became targets in Mexico, Los Aztecas would house them safely in El Paso.

Los Aztecas perfectly exemplified the binational nature of organized crime. It wasn't just that Mexicans and Mexican-Americans teamed up inside the Texas prisons, but that, once back on the streets, they made criminal use of the international divide, including kidnapping people north of the border and taking them to Juárez to kill them and dump the bodies where they were less likely to be found or identified. In 2008, a gang member testified to an El Paso judge that Los Aztecas received drug shipments from a Juárez resident named Eduardo Ravelo, nicknamed El Tablas (the Paddle), who himself received orders from someone referred to as J.L., a deputy of Vicente Carrillo. The same witness testified that Los Aztecas offered their services to the Vicente Carrillo Cartel if they lost a shipment or if there were any problems with clients; Los Aztecas were known for being able to find any enemy (debtors, thieves, traitors, snitches) on either side of the border, having undoubtedly kidnapped and tortured at least one such soul in El Paso. The victim was identified in court as El Chato (Shorty) Flores, a "*carnal*" or blood-brother, as Los

Aztecas called their own members. Members of his own gang kidnapped him in August of 2005 because they suspected him of robbing merchandise worth millions of dollars. The witness said he saw El Chato tied and gagged in a house on the east side of El Paso, where a third individual arrived, accusing El Chato of also having lost a shipment. El Tablas ordered the witness to take El Chato to Juárez and interrogate him. He was later found murdered, the witness admitted.

Los Aztecas originally formed in the mid 1980s and were mostly made up of Mexican-Americans from El Paso, serving time in the southeast Dallas Coffield Prison, where gang affiliation was necessary in order to survive the extreme racial tensions. Putting their mantra, "Aztecas to the death," into practice, the gang spent the next twenty years fighting to extend their influence within various prisons and—by targeting prisoners who were discharged or deported—Juárez itself. Soon they had worked themselves into every sort of criminal undertaking, from drug sales to drug trafficking to auto theft, mostly in Juárez's downtown historic district but also on the west side. Both in Cereso prison and on the streets, Azteca gang members were identified by their short buzz-cuts and the thick, mostly pre-Hispanic-themed tattoos covering their bodies: pyramids, plumes, the words "Barrio Azteca," the letters BA, or the number 21, corresponding to the position of the two letters in the alphabet. It was from within the Texas prisons that they developed their diehard hatred of their rival gang, Los Mexicles (the self-claimed "pure-bred Mexicans"), who splintered off from another Texas prison gang and then crossed the border into Juárez, where they quickly started filling up prisons south of the border. The biggest differences between the two gangs in Cereso were the almost militaristic structure Los Aztecas employed, defining their ranks by captains and soldiers, and the importance they gave to maintaining a sharp appearance and strict personal hygiene, whereas Los Mexicles, the majority of whom were heroin addicts, lived in the filthiest and poorest areas of the prison.

Los Aztecas, with an estimated 1,300 members, were in the majority. Aside from the buildings abutting the prison's criminal courts, where Ward 16 was located, Los Aztecas occupied the entire west wing of Cereso. Los Mexicles, with a mere 300 members, were located on the opposite side of the prison, facing the sierra. In late 2005, with the announcement of the new prison enforcement plan, Los Indios (another name for Los Aztecas) began to wage war against Los Mexicles, turning Cereso into something like a makeshift weapons factory, producing spears, shanks, clubs, and even rudimentary firearms.

Los Artistas Asesinos, who at the time had fewer than a hundred members, were kept locked away under high security in Ward 16 and, except for isolated incidents, were not involved in the bloody brawls of the other two gangs. In an interview with reporter Javier Saucedo, one Double A (Artista Asesino) member said that his gang was different from the other gangs, wanting to keep a low profile. While Los Aztecas and Los Mexicles originally came from Texas, Los Artistas Asesinos were pure Juárez product, children of the maquila boom and witnesses to the crushing violence brought by industrialization and the expansion of the Carrillo Fuentes Cartel. They were young, but they were street tough and had already proven themselves to be killers. They had one other characteristic that set them apart from even the most ruthless of gangs: consequences didn't mean a thing to them.

Vicente fell in easily with the gang of Ward 16. Most members of Double A, Vicente included, saw themselves as having been wounded in their childhood, lacked emotional feeling, were violent and had little respect for human life. They were so sure their past crimes proved them to be as dangerous or even more dangerous than Los Aztecas that they didn't feel the need to show off in the adult prison. Like Vicente, a number of the younger men in Ward 16 had come straight from the School of Social Improvement for Minors and thus had shorter sentences. On the second anniversary of the murder of his family, Vicente explained to Saucedo that a brawl could tack another felony on his record and prolong his stay, which is why he generally tried to stay out of trouble. "The only thing I want is to finish my sentence and get out of here," Vicente said.

That year, 2006, with the protection of the state and local authorities, the Carrillo Fuentes Cartel continued to enjoy almost complete control of the drug-trafficking market in Juárez. The key term here is *almost*. There already existed a small fraction of police and civilian traffickers who were starting to push drugs for the Sinaloa Cartel, headed by Joaquín Guzmán Loera. Known as El Chapo, the Sinaloan had escaped from a maximum-security prison in Jalisco in January of 2001, during the first days of President Vicente Fox's administration. According to various sources, the Sinaloa Cartel was working the market with the help of officials such as ex–State Judge Sergio Garduño Escobedo, who had also worked as chief of the state attorney general's Department of Apprehensions, but who had left his post shortly before the Las Acequias scandal in February 2004. The two cartels began their battle for control of the city soon after the murder of Rodolfo, El Niño de Oro (the Golden Child), the younger brother of Carrillo Fuentes, who was killed in Culiacán, Sinaloa, in September 2004 by hitmen allegedly following orders from El Chapo.

Months after the riots in Cereso, authorities reported that, both inside and outside of jail, members of Los Mexicles were working as peddlers and hitmen for the Sinaloa Cartel and that, at least since 2006, the cartel had been sending "recruiting cells" of killers and traffickers who were finding fertile ground in the teenagers of Juárez's southeastern gangs, where Los Artistas Asesinos had forged tenuous control. The new alliance between Los Mexicles and the Sinaloa Cartel cemented them both as enemies of Los Aztecas. The rivalry didn't take long to tear through Cereso, especially through Ward 16, where, in June 2006, shanks, clubs, metal bars and spears were being used in fights between Double A and a new group of inmates calling themselves Los Guerreros del Diablo (the Devil Warriors), who had allied themselves with Los Aztecas and were fighting for trafficking control in the prison. This time the guards quickly smothered the riot, but the newly minted rivalry put, for the first time, Los Artistas Asesinos on the front lines in the fight against the Carrillo Fuentes Cartel.

These were the tensest months in the history of Cereso. Overcrowded conditions and rumors that prison officials were supporting Los Aztecas in expanding their control of Cereso led to an unprecedented number of complaints made by inmates' family members. They denounced that their relatives had to pay in cash to use any "recreational" area of the prison (patios, athletic fields, even the factory), that they were suffering constant death threats while weapon sales were openly soaring and other inmates enjoyed an unaccountable freedom to travel between cells, hallways and even to different wards. In June 2007, near the end of Murguía's term in office, family members of Los Mexicles again flooded the media with complaints when hundreds of Los Aztecas were let into the wing of Los Mexicles, the day ending in mass bloodshed. The current Cereso warden, the sixth in the last three years, was Fernando Romero Magaña, a childhood friend of Murguía who was frequently involved in illicit activity: accused of watering down liquor in a club (commonly mixing ether or pure alcohol into brand-name bottles) as well as letting narco traffickers retrieve a loot-filled vehicle from a parking lot he owned. Facing further accusations of protecting Los Aztecas, Magaña cried innocent, claiming that it was Los Mexicles who had initiated the June brawl. Security camera footage, however, captured images of Mexicles trying to escape dozens of Aztecas chasing them into Ward 3. There was also footage of a guard signaling a group of Aztecas to attack. Other guards were caught dodging out of the way of charging Aztecas as they raced through the patio and broke into Ward 3. In a screenshot on the patio you can see the dead body of the first of two victims, both of whom died of gunshot wounds. Eleven other prisoners were wounded from gunshots that day. Murguía would later quote his friend Magaña in attributing the violence to overcrowding, publically stating that, given the current conditions, the prisoners ruled Cereso "on their own."

By the end of 2007, with the hegemony of the Juárez Cartel and La Línea crumbling and the entire city collapsing with it, Los Aztecas would lose control of Cereso. Los Aztecas, as members would later testify in El Paso courts, knew that the Sinaloa Cartel would fight the Juárez Cartel for control of the city: it was a rivalry festering since the Las Acequias investigation and catalyzed by El Chapo's alleged murder of El Niño de Oro.

The upsurge of violence in 2007 could already be seen in numbers: according to data compiled by *El Diario*, there were 320 murders that year in Juárez. In the last months of the year, a man described as looking like a "cholo" (gangster), presumably a member of Los Aztecas, killed a police officer dressed in civilian clothing and waiting in line to pay a phone bill. This was perhaps the first in a series of police murders revealing that the old status quo of police protection was no longer binding.

The intensity of violence was registered in the dozens of newspaper articles reporting how crime and corruption had reached shocking levels even for Juárez. Murders attributed to organized crime, as well as so-called common murders, were being committed with increasing frequency. On December 18, a woman was stabbed to death and set on fire. The next day, her body, still burning, was discovered in an empty plot on the west side of Juárez, shortly after somebody reported seeing a two-year-old boy wandering around by himself. The next day, a truck driver was shot to death while driving in the neighborhood of Satélite. Hours later, a twenty-two-year-old man was stabbed to death in the neighborhood of Chaveña, and the following day there were two unrelated murders committed almost simultaneously, one man shot to death outside of a mall and another killed during a liquor store robbery. Later that day, a body was found with signs of having been tortured, an amputated finger discovered in the victim's mouth. The body was later discovered to be ex–Police Sergeant Saulo Reyes Gamboa, who had also worked as a bodyguard for Héctor Murguía. The next day, two bodies were discovered in an empty lot off the side of Highway 2, and the following day a man was found in the neighborhood of Salvárcar, beaten to death and with his head wrapped in tape. That day, the state prosecutor stated that the woman whose incinerated body was found still smoking was originally from Juárez but had been living in New Mexico, and that she'd been killed on the US side of the border by an American with whom she refused to have sexual relations and who then disposed of her body in Juárez. The child found wandering by himself near the body, it was confirmed, was her son. He had witnessed the murder and was then taken by the killer, along with his mother's body, and dumped in Juárez.

By the beginning of 2008, between the general violence and violence connected to extortion and drug trafficking, another unprecedented wave of murders had descended upon Juárez. Always attuned to statistics, *El Diario* reporter Armando Rodríguez noted just how much violence in the city had skyrocketed in the first two weeks of the new year. "24 Murders in 14 Days; Zero Arrests," read the front-page headline of *El Diario* on January 15. "Twelve victims in just the past two days," the article detailed. The last three victims were killed the previous day in what would be the first of many multiple-homicide crimes of the year. "Yesterday at 4:30 AM at the cross streets of Zafra and De la Cruz … three people were shot to death with a hail of 'goathorn' gunfire," Armando wrote. The victims were aged eighteen, twenty-one and seventeen. The last two were brothers. "The officers found three male victims shot to death on the dirt road … The first victim suffered six gunshots to the thorax, the second was shot in the left eye, and the third had multiple gunshot wounds in the legs. The state officers are following various leads on the case. One such lead is that the murder was the result of an inter-gang fight." Armando added that yet another murder had been committed in the southeastern neighborhood of Eréndira, where a thirty-year-old man was found shot to death. "The man's neighbors state that the murder occurred in a small shop known to covertly sell drugs." Among the victims of the first weeks of the year was a three-year-old girl killed by a stray bullet, supposedly fired in celebration of the new year; a twenty-year-old female student at the Tecnológico de Juárez College, originally from Michoacan, sexually assaulted and then stabbed to death on January 1; a prisoner shot to death in Cereso three days later; three men murdered the following day, just eight hours later, one of whom was a *yonkero* (junk dealer) shot to death outside of his storefront and in front of his wife; plus two suicides on the first weekend of the year, the same weekend in which a body was found shot to death and abandoned in a vehicle in the city's Central Park. "Inside the car, music was still playing and the motor was left running," Armando wrote.

The day Armando published the article about the twenty-four murders in the first two weeks of the year, two more people were murdered, and the following day, Tuesday, January 15, Armando wrote another article citing State Attorney General Patricia González, who declared that there was a gang of murderers from the mountains of Chihuahua running amok in the city and employed by "a criminal organization from Sinaloa," referring to the cartel headed by El Chapo. That following day, January 16, undercover federal agents arrested Saulo Reyes in El Paso as he was in the midst of coordinating a shipment of nearly half a ton of marijuana. In the four days following the detention of the ex-official (who seemed very calm on camera), there was a series of attacks against the Chihuahua Police Force, which for years had been protecting the narcos, effectively launching the cartel war for control of Juárez.

It was still dawn on January 20 when the municipal police captain, Julián Cháirez Hernández, thirty-seven years old, was murdered by a gunman who fired twenty-four times at the squad car driving on Plutarco Elías Calles Avenue, approaching Hermanos Escobar Avenue, and only 500 yards from the Rio Grande River. Hernández was shot with 5.7 caliber, 28-millimeter bullets, capable of penetrating bulletproof vests and helmets. Hernández had been a policeman since 1993 and commanded the Aldama Station in Central Juárez. His brother, Ismael Cháirez, also a policeman, was killed in May of the previous year by two AK-47 shots as he was walking to the prosecutor's office on Manuel Gómez Morín Avenue. In an *El Diario* article about the murder, Armando wrote that Saulo Reyes, along with Murguía's secretary of public security, Marco Torres, was, suspiciously, at the scene of the crime during the shooting and could not explain why he was not in his office during regular business hours. At the site of the murder, which was just feet from the Cuauhtémoc Police Station, witnesses identified a green vehicle in which one of the shooters was seen driving away. Minutes later, a green truck was found abandoned nearby. The green 1997 Suburban turned out to be owned by Romero Magaña, the warden of Cereso, who was caught in a public scandal after being called to defend himself before the public prosecutor's office for allegedly protecting Los Aztecas, though he was never charged. As State Attorney General Patricia González would later explain, their investigation focused on the many accounts in which officials who were victims of organized crime were also involved in organized crime. Ismael Cháirez, the police officer killed a few months before, was found to have $1,736 in his pocket. Revealing the find to the public, González added: "I believe it's quite clear that when our own justice officers engage in illicit activities, this is their destiny."

The day after the murder of Julián Cháirez, January 21, 2008, at 7:44 AM, the director of the municipal police of Juárez, Francisco Ledesma, thirty-four years old and already a fifteen-year veteran, also widely known to be intimately involved in gang activity throughout the city, was murdered in his car, in front of his wife and right outside of his house in the Morelos I neighborhood. Dressed in his police uniform, his body, left slumped forward in his 1996 Ford Expedition, was riddled with thirty-five AK-47 bullet wounds. Thirteen hours later, at 8:40 PM of the same day, the first commander of the state public prosecutor's Northern Investigative Unit, Fernando Lozano, was shot while driving his bulletproofed Jeep Cherokee on Paseo Triunfo de la República, very near the Institute of Architecture, Design and Art of the Autonomous University of Juárez. At least five shooters followed Lozano and fired at least fifty shots from separate vehicles. Wounded in the chest by two bullets that had managed to break through his armored car, Lozano survived the attack and was transferred by ambulance across the border to El Paso. Minutes later, 500 troops from the Mexican army stationed in the local garrison began patrolling the streets of Juárez in armored Humvees.

Two days later, an article published in *El Diario* reported that state authorities attributed the attacks on the police to El Chapo's Sinaloa Cartel, whose leaders had decided to do away with the police protection bestowed upon the Carrillo Fuentes Cartel so that they could confront them head on in a fight for absolute control of Juárez. Their strategy was simple: provoke a series of internal conflicts in the ranks of their enemies. The article stated: "Apparently, a few days earlier, people working for El Chapo, including Ismael Zambada, also known as El Mayo, approached police captains from different stations to offer them money in exchange for collaboration … The captains, however, immediately rejected the offer, provoking veiled threats." The article quoted an official at the prosecutor's office, who, referring to officers working for El Chapo, said, "'Nobody is going to tell you whether or not they accepted an offer from Los Chapos, but everybody in the force knows that the three attacks aren't isolated, that there are going to be many more, and everybody is nervous and scared.'" The article was published anonymously.

The environment at the state public prosecutor's office of the Northern Zone had irrevocably changed. Even those who were working for organized crime groups no longer knew who was with which cartel. In the middle of the growing chaos, the only thing that was clear was that the attacks of January 21, followed by the army's takeover of the streets, signaled the beginning of out-and-out war for the Juárez market. For those who doubted it, on the morning of January 26 a group of masked men riding in a dark truck left a wreath of flowers with a sign at the foot of the Monument for Fallen Police Officers on the Juan Gabriel thoroughfare. Written by hand on white cardboard were the words: "For Those Who Didn't Believe: Cháirez, Romo, Baca, Cháirez and Ledesma." All of whom had been assassinated, in that order. The sign had another warning, "For Those Who Still Don't Believe," followed by a list of seventeen officers. Along with 200 other police officers killed in the next two years, six of the men threatened on the cardboard sign were murdered; the surviving eleven eventually fled the city. One of the so-called targets who remained in town survived a shootout in 2008 before finally abandoning the city. He was a friend of Ledesma and was considered the police expert on Los Aztecas.

The Cereso prison branch of the Juárez Cartel didn't stay on the sidelines of the battle. The prisoner killed in the bloody brawl of January 3 was a forty-four-year-old member of Los Aztecas; another seventeen members were severely wounded in the fight. Without the protection of city officials, the two-year-long supremacy of Los Aztecas in Cereso was beginning to fracture, and the once seemingly invincible prison gang was soon crushed. Their most dangerous rivals, however, were not Los Mexicles, who for months were their targets in the bloody war for control of the prison, but the young men barely out of adolescence, mostly jailed for homicide and housed in Ward 16. The fatal brawl erupted at six o'clock the evening of Thursday, January 3, when a number of Double A members were caught climbing the fence separating Ward 16 from Building M, where the women were held, in what seemed like an attempt to break out of the prison. Minutes later, however, on the silent screens of the security cameras, guards watched as dozens of prisoners with clubs and covered faces savagely beat a group of Aztecas. Guards eventually responded by firing tear gas canisters from watchtowers, breaking up the fight and even choking the nearest residents of the Barranco Azul neighborhood out of their homes. But the fighting didn't stop. Double A members set up barriers to the entrance of their ward and were seen carrying firearms, which, according to later investigations, had been manufactured by an ex-soldier in the Mexicles-dominated Ward 4. As the brawl wore on, Los Aztecas scaled the walls in an effort to escape, only to get caught by Los Artistas Asesinos, who took their first victim, shooting Miguel Rueda in the back, a prisoner who was serving the final week of his sentence for robbery. Rueda had been recruited into Ward 11 by Los Aztecas; he showed his affiliation with three new tattoos of pre-Hispanic design. Rueda's cousin, in an interview a few days later, said, "We know he made mistakes. He wasn't in there [Cereso prison] because he was a good or honorable guy. But nobody should be the master of anyone else's life, and nobody should be able to take away a life like this." The cousin ended her statement with an ominous prediction: "If things don't change in Cereso, then I don't know what's going to happen, because he's not going to be the last [victim]."

As new allies of the Chapo-led Sinaloa Cartel, both in the prison and on the streets, Los Artistas Asesinos confirmed their death rivalry with Los Aztecas with the killing of Miguel Rueda. The young gang members were soon swelling with pride. Los Indios (another name for Los Aztecas) couldn't fend off their attacks as they had done with Los Mexicles, proving to the Double A that the rival gang could indeed be conquered. It was around this time that Vicente León, now twenty years old, got his first tattoo: the name of the gang he was living with in the prison ward where he was supposedly being rehabilitated: "Artista" on the left inner forearm and "Asesino" on the right. Each word was about ten inches long and an inch wide. Soon afterwards, the interlaced letters "ASA"—seven inches long and three and a half wide—were tattooed across his chest. Despite his inked affiliation, however, Vicente kept away from the prison brawls, going back to his studies and even taking up his high school equivalency classes again. Officially, however, he was now part of a deadly gang and continued to show signs of being highly dangerous. After an interview with Vicente on January 23, the prison psychologist determined that the young man showed no possibility of social integration, or even interest in such a step. His classification of Vicente as a prisoner of "maximum danger" necessitated his transfer to a maximum-security prison. This would happen to dozens of other Cereso prisoners after their participation in brawls, or even simply as a preventative measure. The psychologists' recommendations, however, were not heeded, and furthermore, in mid 2008, with less than a year left in Vicente's sixty-month prison term, he received news that he was going to be sent back to the School of Social Improvement for Minors. The impetus was the new Law of Specialized Justice for Adolescent Offenders, which was introduced along with the Judicial Reform and, starting July 1 of the same year, ensured that those who committed crimes as minors served their sentences apart from those who committed crimes as adults.

In July 2008, in a patrol car escorted by various other police vehicles, Vicente was transferred across a city that was in open warfare (at this point in the year there had been 540 murders, and 1,500 soldiers were patrolling the streets) to the School in the Carlos Chavira neighborhood on the southeastern edge of Juárez. The School had been moved to a new building, as its previous locale on the edge of the Rio Grande (where Vicente had served an earlier part of his sentence) had been swept away by floods in 2006. The same floodwaters destroyed the original paperwork documenting his parricide. The report of his 2008 transfer (which was partially redacted) described not only that Vicente had had no contact with family members but that none of the relevant parties agreed with his relocation to a juvenile detention facility. The maternal side of the family, according to the document, even worried about their own safety. They were concerned that when Vicente completed his sentence he would come after his younger brother, C.E., who had been living with his grandparents and aunt and uncle since the day after the crime. The family even blamed Vicente for the death of his grandfather, who died in 2007 after mourning for three years the loss of his only daughter.

Administration officials at the School had reservations about the newly returned inmate. Interviews with Vicente concluded that he was still a highly dangerous prisoner and, even more problematic, that given his age and gang affiliation, as well as having survived the worst years of Cereso, he could be looked up to by the younger inmates and thus "gravely" interfere in their process of rehabilitation. They also pointed out that Vicente seemed to show no evidence of wanting to change his antisocial behavior, that he hadn't improved over the course of his years in prison, that he lacked feelings of responsibility, that he was incapable of establishing positive social relationships, that he couldn't control his impulses and that punishment was insufficient to motivate him to change. In conclusion, they saw themselves as dealing with a person unable to feel guilt.

In another report made during his entry into the new prison, administrators exhaustively documented his tattoos and also found Vicente to be addicted to marijuana and cocaine. He had had zero contact with his family or with anybody at all outside of prison in his four years of confinement. Prison officials thus made note of the fact that soon after his transfer Vicente was visited at the School by a few men who arrived in luxury pickup trucks, offering to help him with "whatever he needed." Following the visit, a police officer also came to speak with Vicente, falsely claiming to be a family member.

Vicente wasn't happy about having to leave Cereso. Having to fight for his life inside the adult prison contrasted sharply with the relative calm that reigned among the minors now surrounding him. Further psychological assessments, perhaps alienating him even more, diagnosed Vicente with: superior intelligence compared with the other inmates, a love of excitement left unfulfilled in his new place of confinement, a marked exhibitionism and a need for recognition. The opportunity to prove his leadership came soon after his transfer, when a group of adolescents attempted to provoke a brawl and Vicente, though he hadn't participated, stuck his neck out to receive punishment along with the other troublemakers. The psychologists, who were now meeting with Vicente on a weekly basis, understood this act as an attempt to consolidate his position in the inmate hierarchy and gain respect. In a later report, however, prison officials warned that Vicente's attitude came not out of solidarity with the other prisoners but from his need to reaffirm his position of superiority: he was only interested in others insofar as they could further his own ends. Vicente, the psychologists continued, wanted to leave a good impression, though in the end he was "not very deep, not trustworthy, self-centered, cold, superficial, and incapable of developing friendly relations with others." His psychologists tried to convince him of the benefits of change, but they were supposedly unable to access his emotions. Vicente, they found, once again hid inside himself, engaging in his surroundings just enough to minimally complete his required activities, such as GED classes, carpentry and computer classes, where he learned to use programs like Excel, Word and PowerPoint. His most reliable escape turned out to be literature, and he showed himself to be a smart reader, picking up on important themes in all the books he read. In the following months, he read nearly a book a week, including *Wuthering Heights*, *Women*, *Clubs and Stigmas in the Juárez Nightlife*, *Frankenstein* and *Prisoner of Truth*, a biography of the English philosopher and mathematician Bertrand Russell. Vicente soon began to realize how much he liked to rationalize and that his capacity to calculate proved his marked intelligence. What he didn't like was that the psychologists constantly asked him about his mental capacity, insisting that he was trying to manipulate those around him, or that he gravitated toward the minors who were the most undisciplined.

The year of 2009 arrived with increased anxiety. At twenty-one years old, Vicente was absorbed in his pending release as well as the psychologist's nagging reports. His release was scheduled for May 21, and while the idea of being a free man excited him, he was also deeply worried. He knew he would be vulnerable and that there would be few opportunities for him in a city that, although considered the most violent in Mexico, hadn't yet forgotten Vicente as one of its most notorious murderers: the teenage parricide. Most people figured that he'd be contracted by one of the cartels as soon as he was released. Vicente, who never mentioned his relationship with Los Artistas Asesinos to the psychologists, did say in one of his sessions that he'd like to get out of Juárez, that he'd never be able to find a job, and that he feared for his life. Los Aztecas, who in 2008 had been almost completely wiped out by the Mexican army, had kicked off their counteroffensive, proving their murderous vein by masterminding some of the most brutal crimes Juárez had yet to see. Among their victims, the majority of whom were members of Los Mexicles or Los Artistas Asesinos, were the twenty Cereso prisoners murdered on March 4 when Azteca "soldiers," lists of inmates in hand, pulled Mexicles and Artistas Asesinos out of their cells, beat them, impaled them, sliced their necks and even hung some of their bodies from the fourth-floor balcony. El Dream, long-time prisoner in Ward 16 and a recent convert to Christianity, was the first of the prisoners to be murdered.

Though Vicente's pending release into a war zone surely occupied much of his thoughts, he refused to talk about it with psychologists. Once again, he started losing sleep. In the four years since the violence of Juárez had first convinced him that human life had neither worth nor meaning, the murder rate had multiplied exponentially. But he didn't apply this scorn of life to himself. He lamented his future as a Double A, sworn to a life of murder and crime and released into the violent streets where ranking gang members would see him as nothing but cannon fodder in the battle against the blood-thirsty Aztecas. The self-control that he had developed in Cereso in order to survive soon devolved into what psychologists described as erratic and unpredictable behavior. One day he told them that he wanted to leave the city and the next he didn't know what he wanted to do. Sometimes he wanted to keep studying, find a career, but then that idea failed to satisfy. He wanted to be free, but at the same time this scared him. The dilemmas he faced seemed never-ending, and, at twenty-one years old and nearly five years after killing his parents and his little sister, Vicente León began for the first time to feel like a victim himself. He was tired of the psychologists asking him over and over about his future plans or for details about the gang whose name he had tattooed on his arms. He felt that he simply couldn't respond.

Not everybody at the School, however, thought Vicente was nothing but a danger. Óscar Rodríguez, the sports coach and spiritual advisor for the inmates, found Vicente to be extraordinarily intelligent and figured that with the proper guidance he could have stood out as a contributing member of society even more than he stood out as a criminal. Rodríguez was patient with Vicente, meeting with him every Saturday for two hours of Bible study and consistently surprised at the young man's critical reading capabilities. He found him to be the only inmate who would read the text not literally or in order to memorize it but to use its lessons in order to reflect on his own life. He admired Vicente for his seriousness and discipline despite the chaos of his surroundings. One day toward the end of April 2009, Rodríguez found Vicente alone in the yard and asked him if he would present the next Bible reading in the Saturday class. At the session the following day, Vicente surprised the group by telling them that he had never felt comfortable with them but that the passage that he had decided to read corresponded perfectly to the emotions he was feeling at the moment. He read and presented on a verse from the gospel of Matthew 6:6. "But when you pray, go into your room, close the door and pray to your Father, who is unseen. Then your Father, who sees what is done in secret, will reward you."

His identification with the reading moved him enough so that, with just a few days left in his sentence, he decided that he would continue with his spiritual studies. He liked to consider, he told the rest of the group, that he was alone in a desert, trying to work out the conflicts of his life. In the last days of his imprisonment he gained confidence and even agreed to participate in an inmate talent show. Vicente wanted to confront his fears and decided that the best way to do so would be to offer himself to the public: he signed up to sing. His old friend Eduardo—who at this point had gained permission to visit his parents—used to sing as well. In one of his last days at the School, Vicente took up a guitar and, in front of the small crowd, sang a song whose innocence contrasted not only with his scratchy, deep voice, but also with his past. Nervous at first but soon relaxing, he sang "La Marcha de las Letras" ("The March of the Letters"), by Mexican musician Francisco Gabilondo Soler (Cri-Cri), and even started smiling as the song went on, feeling that he was achieving something, it seemed, with each chord he struck. After the song was over, Rodríguez later recalled, Vicente stood up in front of the applauding inmates and thanked them for their attention, saying that he had just conquered one of his biggest fears.

These are the opening lyrics from "The March of the Letters":

> That one and all leave their books wide open
> the General has given the command.
>
> That all the children pay attention
> and watch the five vowels march right along.
>
> First comes along the letter "A" (*aaah*)
> with its legs long-stepping to carry you on.
>
> Next is the letter "E" (*eeee*) lifting its feet
> with a bar in between that's short and neat.

9

RUPTURES

The following occurred a little after 1:30 AM on Wednesday March 1, 2006, in the southern stretch of Ciudad Juárez. Two vehicles were driving southbound when one of them, a black 2006 Jeep Grand Cherokee without plates, rammed an old maquiladora transport bus. Though the Cherokee was armored, the sheer speed at which it was barreling down Tecnológico Avenue when it hit the bus, which was just starting to nose across the avenue on Delicias Street, resulted in a crash that instantly killed one of the Cherokee's passengers. The cream leather interior of the vehicle was torn, stained with blood. The front of the bus, meanwhile, was utterly destroyed, the motor shot, the hood blown off, the windows shattered and the metal body twisted so violently over the passengers that one was killed and the driver suffered injuries from which he would never completely recover. In the state prosecutor's preliminary report 5533/2006, written for the two incidental murders eventually pinned on the bus driver, the investigating agents reported that the driver of the Cherokee was "helped by two persons from another vehicle who took him to get medical attention," though they were "unable to obtain further information from the wounded man." The two unidentified persons took the driver of the Cherokee to the hospital, Poliplaza Médica, arriving at 2:38 AM and leaving immediately, without even explaining to the medics how the man had been injured. The space allotted to the man's name in the preliminary report was left blank—investigators explained the omissions by claiming that the passengers were unable to procure "such information given the late hour at which the accident occurred."

The only person at the scene of the accident who was interviewed by investigating agents was the driver of the "rutera," the mini-bus registered as number 7304. The driver was a forty-five-year-old Oaxacan who, exhausted, had just finished a circuit of his route, dropping off employees at the maquila compound Lear Corporation and, unfortunately for him as well as for all of Juárez, ran a stop sign and drove the 1989 bus into the oncoming traffic of Tecnológico Avenue, directly into the path of the speeding black Cherokee. Interviewed as he lay bandaged in the Family Hospital of downtown Juárez, the driver said he had been opening the passenger door of the bus to let somebody in when he was smacked with the stick shifter. He claimed, however, not to have seen who it had been he was trying to open the door for. This unidentified person, it would turn out, shot him in the arm, though the driver claimed that he had lost consciousness and didn't come to until he was in the ambulance, not realizing he had been shot until later. "That's it," he said. "I don't remember anything else that happened … I didn't see anybody's face and I don't remember anything."

Perhaps it was best for the driver not to remember what he

said not to have even seen that morning. Luckily for him, the investigators didn't ask many questions either. It was reported that the bus driver had been shot inside his vehicle, but the case files didn't identify the driver or passengers of the other vehicle, those who, according to *El Diario*, were armed and part of a caravan that included a cherry-red Dodge Durango and a white Cherokee. The deceased victim, left on the pavement next to the black Cherokee, was a big man, six feet two inches tall, dark-skinned, with a military-style crew cut and dressed in jeans, suede shoes and an orange dress shirt. He'd been riding shotgun without a seatbelt and ended up halfway thrown out of the vehicle. He was later identified as Jaime Magdaleno Flores, a Juárez "businessman," thirty-two years old and living in the Morelos II neighborhood. He had been a Juárez police officer from 1994 to 2005, and, despite having been one of the principal suspects in the kidnapping of two police captains—one of whom had been his patrol partner— he had retired in good standing one year before the accident.

The last effort taken in investigating the case—in order to ascertain whether anyone else rode in the black Cherokee with Magdaleno Flores, instead of taking the bus driver's pitifully incomplete declaration at face value—was an attempt to interview the man who, the morning after the accident, showed up at the house of the Flores family to tell them that his ex-colleague had been killed. The man's name was Jorge Baca; he was thirty years old and had been an inactive police officer since 1997. Investigators, however, failed to locate him for questioning, and a year and a half later, in November 2007, he was shot and killed at point-blank range by a member of Los Aztecas in the plain light of day inside a cell phone company's customer service center. That very day, the

Durango, the same one that had rescued the passengers from the black Cherokee, was spotted outside of the cell phone company building in the parking lot of the Galerías Tec mall. Baca's name was third down on the list of "those who didn't believe," as sprayed on the narco-poster on January 26, 2008. His nickname was, somewhat confoundingly, El Cuarto (the Fourth).

Baca and the others in the black Cherokee were armed to the teeth on the night of the accident. They were driving full speed in a caravan with Juárez's de facto drug-trafficking boss, Dos Letras (Two Letters), J.L. He was the young Sinaloan who first came to town as an ordinary hitman and was, at only thirty-four years old, already the right-hand man of Vicente Carrillo Fuentes. J.L.'s most defining traits were his complete loyalty to the organization and his capacity to maintain La Línea, the largest network of protection and executioners the city had ever seen, made up of both police and ex-police, like those who had murdered the victims discovered in Las Acequias, or those who were traveling with him on the night of the accident.

The nickname J.L. first appeared in the Juárez media in 2004, after an American informant tied to the Las Acequias debacle called him out as head of operations of the Juárez Cartel, as well as probable mastermind behind the twelve murders and hidden burials. Despite being identified (initially by US authorities), J.L. was able to survive and, mostly through weekly payments of hundreds of thousands of dollars—up to $2,000 per policeman per week—to keep officials on all three levels of government at his beck and call. J.L. was also ostensibly responsible for all of the drug shipments—be it by highway, airport or dirt trail—into the state of Chihuahua, as well as charging a tax for all merchandise not belonging to Vicente Carrillo, namely, the drugs of El Chapo, whose grip over Chihuahua had begun to tighten since his escape from Puente Grande prison in 2001. With this broad-stroke territorial domination, J.L. was able to maintain iron-fisted control over drug sales and almost all drug-related business in Juárez, including car theft, a fundamental key to committing hard-to-trace "lifts" as well as murders and drug transfers to the United States.

J.L. was obsessed with achieving total control over the "plaza," a cartel term for a specific geographical market, or "turf." He also enjoyed "combing" Juárez, nearly street by street, in his notorious caravans of armored vehicles, which would later be celebrated in many folk-*corridos*. With his group of bodyguards, made up almost entirely of police and ex-police armed with AK-47s, he would drive down Manuel Gómez Morín Avenue, crossing the valley until the street turned into De la Raza Avenue, tunneling into the heart of downtown, the hub of drug sales. He was often seen on Tecnológico Avenue, where he would host meetings with ex-cops at Capone's, a bar that opportunistically renamed itself after the American gangster only a few days after the discovery of the Las Acequias mass grave. A number of sources testified that the caravans were designed to "lift" either policemen or members of Los Aztecas who were making sales without a nod of approval from the Juárez Cartel. Once they were kidnapped, the "lifted" were taken to safe houses where they were forced to name their sources, their phones were searched, and their merchandise was confiscated. Then they were murdered, often buried outside of random houses like at Las Acequias. Beginning in 2008, the Mexican army was finding more and more bodies in mass graves. Other victims were simply dumped in the street.

Constant presence is how J.L. kept control. It was always obvious when J.L. was on the streets. If his yellow Hummer was parked outside of Mango's, for example, the bar on De la Raza Avenue, it meant J.L. had run out all patrons so he could have the place to himself, his bodyguards perched in the corners. J.L. was brown-skinned, chubby, with puffy cheeks that accentuated his beardless chin and contrasted with his ostentatious display of power and his lack of mercy. The folk songs he inspired spoke of a gold-plated, diamond-studded .38 Super Automatic that bore his initials and was usually tucked into his waistband. One song described his voice as "making the ground tremble." But the songs mostly exalted his cold-bloodedness. His signature execution-style shot to the head. His unexpected wrath—which would come out even against members of his inner circle. That was how Luis Antiga, ex-cop and owner of Capone's, thirty-five years old and one of J.L.'s top men, was killed only twenty days after the car accident: inside his own bar, killed by two masked men with machine guns, shot first in the back, then in the shoulder, the stomach, the heart, four more shots to the head, and the last one right between the eyebrows.

Other nicknames for J.L. were El Loco (the Crazy) or La Bestia (the Beast). Years later he would be named as the mastermind behind nearly half of the thousands of murders committed in Juárez up until the end of 2009. He was so unpredictable that he even dared threaten Vicente Carrillo Leyva, son of Juárez Cartel capo Amado Carrillo, who, in a testimony before the assistant attorney general for special investigations and organized crime, explained that J.L. had chastened him for not following in the footsteps of his father and going into the business. "He's bloodthirsty. He threatened to kill me about two and a half years ago," Vicente testified in March of 2009. He also gave investigators an identifying characteristic: "He limps on one side."

The fallout from the car accident spiked J.L.'s thirst for violence. An anonymous source had seen him in a hospital wrapped in bandages from head to toe, several of his teeth missing. Rivals hoped he would never recover, and some claimed it was the accident that gave him the limp he hated so much and that Vicente Carrillo later mentioned to investigators. After killing the owner of Capone's, he demanded a series of "lifts" and executions, explained by state police as a reshuffling "in the organization of cartels operating on the border," which, in the third week of April 2006, left five victims murdered by shots to the head. J.L. was out of control. Even in his circle many were starting to think that it would have been better if he had died in the accident.

That was what Julio Porras thought. He was a fifty-two-year-old ex–federal policeman who had joined the business in Chihuahua. According to a real estate public registry, he owned an exchange house and a construction company, and he was known to frequent a bar called La Caldera. He also owned a mechanic shop, West Texas Diesel Repair, in El Paso. A witness to a 2010 drug-trafficking case in El Paso identified Porras as El Viejón (the Old Man), the cartel member supposedly in charge of controlling Chihuahua city police.

Porras's problems with J.L. began when he assumed El Loco wasn't going to survive the accident, and he propositioned Vicente Carrillo that he himself replace J.L. in Juárez. Not only did he not get the promotion he was after, but word got back to J.L., and, unsurprisingly, he was furious. J.L.'s first order of business, after "settling his accounts" on the border in April, was to seek vengeance with El Viejón in Chihuahua. On May 19, 2006, the ex-cop was the target of an attack at his house in the San Felipe neighborhood and was able to escape only because he'd been granted bodyguard protection by the local PAN government. Two of the guards, however, were murdered in the attack, and the white Yukon that Porras usually drove was riddled with bullets. The official driving the Yukon that day survived and explained that the ex–chief of police, one of Porras's dedicated followers, had entrusted him with the protection of El Viejón.

Porras's close relationship with the state governor, José Reyes Baeza, was a sore spot among some of the governor's other cabinet members, including State Attorney General Patricia González, who had known the governor since their student days at the law school of the Autonomous University of Chihuahua. Baeza, despite increasing opposition, continued to follow Porras's instructions, bending to his will however he could. An anonymous message sent to various media outlets on May 25 explained that Porras enjoyed such extravagant control of the state government because he'd bought out the governor, the ex-governor and the current senatorial candidate, Fernando Baeza Meléndez. Since 2004, there had been constant tension between much of the state police (hand-picked by Porras) and the state attorney general, Patricia González. Porras also seemed to have differences of opinion with the secretary of public security, Raúl Grajeda Domínguez, a notoriously obese lawyer who received an anonymous death threat purportedly from Porras. Another anonymous note sent to the press warned that Porras was threatening to form a new cartel to fight for domination of the Chihuahua market, still held by the enraged but wounded J.L.

Just as Secretary of Public Security Raúl Grajeda wrote in a book never published but delivered to *El Diario*, once Porras broke with J.L. in May 2006, he fell short of forming a new organization as the anonymous note had warned, but he allied himself with a cartel—the Sinaloa Cartel—that only a few months previously had stopped paying sales taxes to the Juárez Cartel, renewing efforts to strip away their hegemony in Chihuahua. They were ready to fight. Grajeda, who also received an order from Governor Reyes Baeza to obey Porras, described El Viejón as starting to "sell information to the Sinaloa Cartel, which wanted to take advantage of the infighting that, after the car accident, had spread all the way up to the governor's office. "That," Grajeda wrote, "sparked the war between the cartels, the worst narco war that Mexico has ever seen."

Ex–Juárez policeman Jesús Manuel Fierro Méndez offered another view of why Porras left the Juárez Cartel for the Sinaloa Cartel. During his trial in El Paso for distributing more than 1,000 kilos of marijuana, Méndez testified not only that El Viejón had joined forces with El Chapo but that he had leaked information about the Juárez Cartel to US government agents. Fierro Méndez, who for ten years had worked as a cop on the border, admitted to colluding with Ismael "El Mayo" Zambada (second-in-command of the Sinaloa Cartel) and that he and Porras weren't the only ones "who had been working for Vicente Carrillo, and then left to join up with El Chapo." He added that, after an assassination attempt against him, he agreed to collaborate with US ICE agents. His government contact, he claimed, identified himself as the chief of ICE in El Paso. He was being relocated to a different sector and wanted to drop a bombshell so as to be able to stay and finish the investigation he had started. "He was the one," Fierro Méndez concluded, "who had the most info on J.L."

Fierro Méndez explained to the court that El Viejón wanted to replace Dos Letras (another nickname for J.L.) in order to prevent Chihuahua from turning into a bloodbath. According to Méndez, Porras had been "predicting for years what is happening now [in 2010]." Dos Letras would push the cartel to new levels of barbarity.

Which is exactly what happened. In the first months of 2008, the violence sparked by El Chapo's fight with J.L. for control of the Juárez drug market exceeded the limits of imagination. In January, there were forty-six homicides. In February, there were forty-nine. Then 117 in March—the city had become an open battlefield. The war descended into an unprecedented level of savagery, the bloodshed increasingly difficult to understand. Given the lack of official investigation or even plausible explanation, the only clues to the murders were the messages left by the killers themselves: the Sinaloa Cartel was provoking a split in the Juárez Cartel.

So explained a sign—left on the morning of May 23 in an empty lot wedged between a religious school and a maquila— found next to five bodies, two of them decapitated, with their heads, wrapped in black bags, weighing down the sign. The sign read: "This is what happens to fucking traitors who work with the sissy dog-fucker Chapo Guzman who does nothing but guarantee your death, keep sending us more idiots to dispose of. Sincerely, La Línea."

The Sinaloa Cartel responded with a similarly fearless boast: "For the pigs of J.L. You think posting messages and burning people's businesses and wrecking the trade is going win you the market you fucking scabs who don't even realize you're worthless and have never had anything. Where are the officials and agents who kidnap and kill as they please … why don't they show their faces if they're so badass? Where are those friends you bring along for safety? And we're not dog-fuckers. We're pig-fuckers." The banner was hung a few days later, above two AK-47 cartridges, in the parking lot of a shopping mall. At this rate, despite the deployment of 2,000 soldiers to the streets, the bodies were piling up faster than ever. On May 12 alone, there were eight people killed in gunfights throughout the city. One at midnight, another at 3:40 AM, then again at 4:30 AM, then 9:30 AM, again at 2:00 PM, and three more at 3:40 PM.

The FBI identified Los Aztecas as responsible for at least half of the murders committed during this period of the Juárez War. The *Washington Post*, citing government sources, reported that in 2010 Los Indios (Los Aztecas) had become a sophisticated murder-machine, having "honed their ability to locate targets, stalk them and finally strike in brazen ambushes involving multiple chase cars, coded radio communications, coordinated blocking maneuvers and disciplined firepower by masked gunmen in body armor. Afterward, the assassins vanish, back to safe houses in the Juárez barrios or across the bridge to El Paso."

According to the Chihuahua state government, many of the young men violently tearing through the streets were not originally from Los Aztecas but were recruited en masse to work as assassins for the Juárez Cartel. As testimonies of some of the young men charged with multiple homicides described, La Línea contracted groups of men—almost always under thirty years old and from the poorest neighborhoods of Juárez—and charged them with working through lists of people to murder. The groups of assassins were divided according to police sector, and their labor was specialized: some merely cleaned weapons, some found the targets, others were drivers, others—known as hawks—watched the streets for soldiers or enemies, and then there were the shooters, almost always working out of a moving vehicle, drive-by style, though sometimes also breaking into the target's house, eliminating them there. The testimonies, given by multiple subjects under the new judicial process, also described how recruitment worked: "A neighbor invited me to kill some people for money. My first job was to execute a dealer in Riveras del Bravo, a guy who was loaded with cocaine, and so Estrella and I went to see him. Someone else named Perro told us what he looked like and all that, and so Estrella and I got in a Blazer [the vehicle] and we got to where he was supposed to be in Riveras del Bravo. When we rolled up [the target] was standing there. He was wearing a bulletproof vest and black pants. He figured we were going to get him in the truck and hand over some merchandise, since he was a pusher, but when we stopped, Estrella told me to get out. I was packing a forty. I shot him five times, then we went to a safe house and waited there all day. That was when I realized that this was going to be my job, how I was going to get paid." The assassins tended to charge between 2,000 and 5,000 pesos (less than $500) a week for killing between three and twenty people.

Denying that they were connected to La Línea, the suspects —almost all of them from Juárez, mostly the neighborhoods of Azteca, Pradera del Sur, Zaragoza or Salvarcar—claimed to work as refrigerator technicians, used clothes salesmen or various other jobs, earning about 500 pesos (less than $50) a week. Not one of them had a professional career; a few had gone to school only until the third grade.

Although evidence pointed to probable guilt in a few of the cases—a woman told me she recognized her grandson's murderer in photographs the military had published of the suspects—the problem was that the public prosecutor's office was only taking testimonies that had been gathered at the military base, where, according to a number of the suspects, they had been brought after being kidnapped by the Joint Chihuahua Operation (a common practice in interrogations) and submitted to hours of physical and psychological torture.

Without presenting any reliable evidence against the suspects, the army led a systematic campaign to attack the interests of the Juárez Cartel. They started by arresting, almost en masse, members of Los Aztecas, including a group of twenty-one people arrested just a month after the posting of the ominous message for "those who didn't believe" and who were brought to the military base showing signs of having been severely beaten. Next in line were J.L.'s top two underlings. The first was Pedro Sánchez, who for years had run operations in Villa Ahumada (a town halfway between Chihuahua and Juárez), where drugs were stored and shipped to the United States. Pedro Sánchez, alias El Tigre (the Tiger), was detained in Parral on May 13 in a gunfight with soldiers. At the time of his arrest he had on him an ID from the Federal Agency of Investigation (akin to the FBI), given to him by the attorney general's office. On July 10, the army detained Gonzalo García, alias El Chalo, capturing him in a hotel along with the brother of a man who was detained only three days before. With each new detention, another spray of blood hit the pavement. Soon, the state would be flooded.

Just four days after Pedro Sánchez was arrested in Parral, a shootout in Villa Ahumada left six people dead, eight kidnapped and nearly a dozen houses riddled with machine-gun fire. In caravans of trucks with four to six masked men riding in each bed—likely members of the Sinaloa Cartel—they overran the city streets from 11 PM to 3 AM, taking advantage of a temporary retreat of the army. "That was the day we were changing guards, when the soldiers who'd been stationed there went to Chihuahua City and then Mexico City to make room for a new deployment that was going to come in the very next day. That was the night …" General Felipe de Jesús Espitia, chief of the Joint Chihuahua Operation, explained to me.

With 136 murders, May was one of the most violent months in the history of any Mexican city. The coming brutality of the cartel war was even forewarned by two emails circulating in Juárez that month. They warned that between May 23 and 25, citizens would do well to stay off the streets and limit their time spent in public areas. A massacre was coming, heralding the arrival of Joaquín "El Chapo" Guzmán. The US Consulate in Juárez took note of the anonymous emails and posted its own official advisory to US citizens. The warnings had their effect. On the afternoon and evening of Saturday, May 24, the streets were uncannily quiet. I had always thought our passion for nightlife would be the last thing we would cede to our fear, and it was happening that night, with bars and restaurants shuttering early, people recognizing the threat was real. That Friday there were ten murders. Another eight on Saturday. By the end of May, there would be 100 more murders in just that month than in all of 2007. And the violence continued, with 139 murders in June, 146 in July, 228 in August, 118 in September and 181 in October. On the Day of the Dead, November 2, seemingly all of Juárez was in mourning for the 1,200 murders counted so far that year. The whole city was terrified. The warring cartels had set dozens of stores on fire, punishing the business owners who catered to their enemies or who simply couldn't pay an extortion fee, a "crime" that a few years before didn't even exist but that now, along with kidnappings, had become a daily part of the rapidly expanding culture of violence.

Soon we saw the warfare turn even bloodier. The morning of Tuesday, November 4, students of the high school Colegio de Bachilleres 6 found a dead body a few feet from the school entrance on the streets of Manuel Gómez Morín and Faraday, nearly directly in front of the Cuauhtémoc Police Station. The victim had been shot in the head and left in a pool of blood, his face covered by a pig mask. He was later identified, wrote Armando in *El Diario*, as thirty-three-year-old David Cerpa. Written on a banner signed by El Chapo and left near the body: "This is what happens to aztecas who help pigs."

La Línea responded with equal, perhaps even more barbaric ostentation. On the morning of the following Thursday, a bus driver in the same neighborhood discovered a hanging body with its hands tied and its head decapitated. A message attached to it read, "I, Lázaro Flores [owner of Las Anitas Water Park, a man who had already survived a shootout and was known to be renting out his land to the military], support my boss the dog-fucker. Look out Garduño, the Fierro brothers, de la O, and the fucking little Mayans. Sincerely, La Línea." The body was left hanging for three hours, until soldiers shut down traffic in order to take it down. Later, the missing head was found wrapped in a plastic bag in a plaza commemorating journalists, known as Plaza del Periodista, in downtown Juárez.

Four days later, around 6:45 AM, on November 10, the burnt body of a man, with both arms amputated, was dumped in front of the barbwire fence of the Cuauhtémoc Police Station. Along with the two arms, left to one side of the body, the murderers left two lighters and a message: "For La Línea and Los Aztecas. Here's Héctor Calzada, burner of businesses, extortionist, dirty snake for Pablo Ríos Rodríguez and J.L. and Vicente Carrillo. You see pigs? This is how all the snakes disturbing the peace in Juárez are going to end up. Sincerely, Sinaloa Cartel. And this is the market of El Chapo Guzman. P.E. [Pig Exterminator]."

Armando, who, along with a number of other reporters in the city, had received ongoing death threats since January of 2008, wrote the *El Diario* articles about all three incidents, though only naming the responsible cartel in the case of the victim wearing the pig mask. In his following articles, beginning with a piece on the burnt, armless corpse, he did not specify names or cartel affiliations. I'm not sure if it was the head found in the Plaza del Periodista that made Armando think twice about publishing too much information about the narcos. Or maybe it was when Governor José Reyes Baeza, in a speech at the Autonomous University of Juárez shortly after the corpse was discovered in front of the police station, said reporters should avoid being used as "puppets" by organized crime and should only publish the basic facts, "without self-censorship" but "without more information" than necessary about the drug traffickers.

Two days later, on a cold Thursday morning at eight,

outside of his house, while sitting in his white Tsuru car next to his eight-year-old daughter, Armando was murdered. He was shot ten times with a 9-millimeter pistol. The assassin did a professional job. Armando was shot first through the glass of the door window and then through the windshield, most of the shots hitting him in the stomach. Armando, "our beloved Choco," as his wife referred to him in the obituary, was left in the driver's seat, slumped over, with his head tilted slightly to the left, the seeping blood barely perceptible beneath his blue jacket. A photograph from his funeral—his oldest daughter hugging a photo of her father and staring into the distance, a look of profound sadness in her honey-colored eyes—still hangs in the editing room at *El Diario*.

After his murder, *El Diario* republished an article Armando had written on October 29 that, according to the paper, was his "most controversial." Collaborating with a reporter from Chihuahua, he had written about the murder of the nephew of State Attorney General Patricia González. Her nephew, Mario González, was driving a state car (despite not being an employee of the state) when he was abducted. Armando's article also details the political family's history of involvement with narco trafficking, including the story of an in-law caught with thirty-three bundles of cocaine.

Without directly responding to the newspaper's provocation, State Attorney General Patricia González presented the editors with information that named the principal suspect of Armando's murder: an ex–state policeman and member of La Línea whose motive, González claimed, was to silence El Choco after he'd given narco information to another journalist who had recently received political asylum in the United States. González had supposedly obtained the information from an informant who overheard a man boasting about how his father, the ex-cop, had murdered Armando.

Taken from the informant's recording: "I heard the subject say to the young man, the twenty-five-year-old son of the ex-policeman: 'Your pops got in some good punches the other day.' And the son responded, 'Yeah but he really had to give it to that fucking reporter, 'cause he was running his mouth like a bitch. [In Spanish, literally, *acting like a pig's snout*.]'"

The preliminary inquiry of the public prosecutor's office called for an investigation into any links between State Attorney General González and drug traffickers and subpoenaed records of her own investigation into the murder of her nephew. The investigator assigned to the case, José Ibarra Limón, sent a summary of the investigation to *El Diario* claiming that he was weighing "the possibility that certain persons involved in certain acts were also involved in the murder of Armando Rodríguez." A month later, on the night of July 27, Ibarra Limón was murdered, just like Armando, shot to death in front of his house as he was getting out of his truck. His murder, like so many that he himself was investigating, remains unsolved.

Halfway through 2009 and there had already been more than 2,000 murders in the city. It felt like Juárez was drowning in a flood of polluted water: corpses were rotting in the streets, and we had come to expect eight murders a day, the echoing of gunfire, the fear, the general incapacity to understand these dimensions of barbarity—a city where homicide had become one of the most trivial of crimes. Thinking of Vicente León, that if he thought he could kill without consequences in 2004, certainly nobody, no amalgam of institutions, could prepare for what was brewing in the minds of tens of thousands of children who were growing up in the rising plague of violent deaths that had overtaken every facet of the city.

Violence—seething in the darkest corners of our subconscious—had become our outlet for frustration, ready to emerge uninhibited, free of any moral consideration to contain it. Among the thousands of crimes that I had heard and read and written about in the city from 2008 on, there were two that stuck out to me as clear examples of what had happened to our society. The first occurred on January 21, minutes after the murder of police captain and gang expert Francisco Ledesma: in the southeastern neighborhood of Horizontes del Sur, a fifty-eight-year-old man stabbed and hatcheted to death his eight-month-pregnant daughter-in-law and, after committing the crime, drove to Cereso prison to turn himself in to the police because he had just "done something stupid." The victim, left in the bathroom in a pool of blood and with the hatchet still stuck in her skull, was murdered in front of her two children, one of whom, eleven years old, had phoned his father to tell him that grandpa was hitting his mother. When reporters interviewed the murderer, Juan Manuel López, at Cereso prison, he explained that the problem had started the night before, when he and his daughter-in-law got in a fight "about a loveseat." The next day he decided to get revenge.

Less than a month later, at about six in the evening on February 4, the forty-seven-year-old Ismael Carrasco stabbed his ex-mistress to death inside a grocery mart in the southern Juárez neighborhood of Héroes de la Revolución. While they were in the store, Carrasco, his ex, Margarita, and her daughter and son, Verónica and Javier, started arguing. Verónica pushed Carrasco, and her mother tried to intervene in the following tussle, when Carrasco pulled a knife and stabbed her in the head and chest. In the court hearing, after Carrasco had been identified by a cashier—who recounted that the woman approached the checkout line soaked in blood and gripping her stomach—he interrupted the defense of his public attorney and claimed responsibility. "I made a mistake, Your Honor," Carrasco began. "I recognize that, and I feel awful, but I did it because they pushed me so far, insulting me and offending me all the time. I'd like to make clear that this came from a situation that had been going on for months and months. They were never arrested for having robbed and vandalized my house. They made life so impossible, we had to separate. Then they shot up my house. I tried to put my life back together and I never even bothered Margarita, but her family kept on threatening me. In the grocery store, Verónica started nagging at me and then Javier told me I was going to die. They'd already shot up my house, and the police have the records. Javier is a robber and he'd threatened to kill my son."

Vicente León had few options when he was released in May 2009. The profound insecurity set off by the cartel war and its waves of extortion and kidnapping was even further exacerbated by the US economic and mortgage meltdowns in late 2007, which ultimately led to the loss of 100,000 jobs in Chihuahua State, the majority due to maquila closures in Juárez. Local shops were closing so fast that the estimated number of shuttered businesses soon reached 10,000. Tens of thousands of square feet in industrial warehouses were put up for rent or sale. The Institute of Municipal Research and Planning estimated that 100,000 houses and apartments, or nearly a quarter of all housing units, were left empty and abandoned in the city.

Drug trafficking, however, continued to be one of the steady sources of employment. The Sinaloa Cartel, much like La Línea, started forming cells of assassins, setting them up in safe houses throughout the city. From the testimonies of detained suspects, investigators learned that members of Los Artistas Asesinos were living in "offices" in neighborhoods like Hacienda de las Torres or Municipio Libre, in southeastern Juárez. They also used these offices to hide kidnapping victims and to store weapons—in one police raid they found four AK-47s, an AR-15, a smoke grenade and more than 700 cartridges of ammunition. Similar to La Línea's hitmen, the majority of these assassin cells were made up of young men under twenty-five years old who were organized according to job task: some tracked victims, some pulled the trigger, and some kept the "offices" tidy. The pay was also comparable to the rival cartel: about 3,000 pesos a week, or less than $300.

But it wasn't long-term employment. Members of Los Artistas Asesinos were being slaughtered by Los Aztecas—most of them older than the typically teenage or young-adult Double As—at the same rate that Los Aztecas were being wiped out by allies of El Chapo and the Sinaloa Cartel. The prison murder of El Dream and a number of other Mexicles and Artistas Asesinos in March 2009 was a strong and clear message to the "new boys." On July 30, authorities discovered another headless body, this one with charred hands and feet, with a message left next to it: "We're coming after the rest of you kidnappers."

Little is known about how Vicente León filled his time in the three months between his release from the School of Social Improvement for Minors on May 21, 2009, and the night of

August 24, when he met up with Iván Vital Castañón, a young man Vicente's age who had served time for robbery and who was now one of the ringleaders of a local Artistas Asesinos cell. Vital had been released from Cereso only fifteen days before, after being exonerated of yet another charge of robbery. In September 2008, a witness had caught him and some accomplices going into a maquila armed with heavy weapons and attempting to steal a cash register and a forklift when, upon hearing police sirens, the group bolted. The witness, however, retracted his statement a year later in court, leading to Vital's release.

Vital, whose parents were separated (his father lived in El Paso) was locked up in Ward 16 from September 2008 to November 2008, when he was transferred to Cereso prison, where he was lucky enough to survive La Línea's "extermination campaign," which had killed El Dream.

Though Vital was officially unemployed, he had enough resources to dress in style. The night of August 24 he wore a yellow short-sleeved Hollister shirt, Tommy Hilfiger jeans and white Puma sneakers. Vicente was wearing a long-sleeved brown shirt and blue jeans (both generic) and shoes from a Divano catalogue.

Late that night (a little after one in the morning, already August 25) the two young men drove a 1988 Mitsubishi with Chihuahua plates to Ramón Rayón Street, one of the major thoroughfares in the southeastern Papigochi neighborhood of Juárez, where they went to a taco stand named after the Sinaloa city Los Mochis. They sat down at a red metal table stamped with a Coca-Cola logo and had yet to start eating their tacos when two shooters approached them. The young men had no chance to defend themselves. The assassins opened fire at almost point-blank range, shooting at least sixty-five times with .9 and .40 caliber pistols. Vicente's body was left just off the street, on his back, riddled with at least sixteen bullet wounds. The shots perforated his buttocks, both legs, both arms, his chest and nearly destroyed his face. Internally, the bullets perforated his liver, a lung, the small intestine and his heart. At least one bullet tore through his brain, which, according to the autopsy, killed him instantly. Iván Vital suffered nearly the same: fourteen shots destroying his chest, stomach, liver, intestines, face, head and heart. Both of them were left in a puddle of blood. From the force of the initial impacts on his left side, Vicente fell over on that same side, with his right arm, soon to be black from lack of circulation, resting across his bloodied chest. His right leg was similarly thrust over his body and to his left. In the forensic photograph his mouth and eyes were both half-open. Except for an expression of panic, or pain, he looked the same as he did five years earlier when he was just a teenager: high cheekbones, thick eyebrows, light skin, no mustache and a recently shaved head. He was just as thin as before. The police department opened case number 20012, the number of so-called ordinary crimes committed at that point in Juárez in 2009. The case document, as was typical, described in minute detail the physical description of each victim, their wounds and the trajectory of each bullet that tore through their bodies. The case file included two photographs of Vicente in the morgue, his tattoos identifying him as an Artista Asesino, the words inked onto each forearm, as well as the letters, partially erased by bullet wounds, "ASA" on his chest. In the photo, other bodies can be seen behind Vicente, all of them naked and some also riddled with bullets, lying on the metallic benches at the Juárez Laboratory of Medical Forensic Services, which had been filled beyond capacity various times throughout that year.

And that was it. Nobody followed up on the investigation of the teenage parricide that had so shocked Juárez five years previously. Unlike with the murders of his family, nobody else tried to tell his story or ask questions. Maybe the man running the taco stand had seen something, but there was no mention in the report that the police had interviewed him; nor were any other witnesses registered; nor was there any other trace of evidence that could have led to discovering the motive behind the murder or the identities of the murderers. There was no story, no suspect. It wasn't like it had been five years before, when Vicente, as if it were a relief, explained in detail why he had decided to murder his family.

Of Vicente's murder, we know little else but that he ended up on the ground with Iván, between the taco stand and two tables. The same day, August 25, 2009, eleven other people were killed in Juárez, five of them in one incident. By three in the morning there had already been nine victims, including Vicente and Iván.

Iván's older sister learned of his death early the next morning when, while watching the morning news, she recognized her brother's yellow shirt. Along with her father, she came to the morgue to identify her brother's corpse, which was then transferred to El Paso for burial.

Nobody came for Vicente's body. Nearly three months later, after being stored with fifteen other corpses in the city morgue, Vicente León Chávez was buried alone, with no witnesses other than the forensic team who occasionally go to the

San Rafael City Cemetery to bury, in a common grave, those who share Vicente's destiny along the border, almost all of them victims of murder.

10

... AND JUSTICE?

Juan Gabriel is one of the most popular musicians in all of Latin America, and perhaps the most important living composer in Mexico. Raised in poverty, he incarnates one of those tales—so exploited by the media—of how talent and perseverance can lead, even in Mexico, to incredible success. He belts out pop ballads whose lyrics swing between either melancholic or banal and yet, when sung, almost always sound profoundly honest and emotional. What makes his songs hit so hard, I think, are the original arrangements accompanying his lyrics, the unexpected eruption of the trumpets, or how, after a declarative line like "habit is more powerful than love" (which hits home especially hard in Mexico, where we're resigned to the disaster of our social, economic and political surroundings), we're blasted by another dramatic cloudburst of dozens of violins lamenting the cruel inevitability of destiny. His creative interpretations, his dance moves, his *grito*, his love of pleasing his audience, as well as his gay pride, have made him one of the most beloved artists in the past half century across all Mexican classes. I can confidently say that thousands and thousands of us are able to mark an important moment in our lives, or in our loves, with a few choice phrases from Juan Gabriel.

One of my Juan Gabriel moments came when I was five years old (I'm now forty-one, and I grew up with his music), accompanied by the song "En esta primavera" ("This Spring"), in which Gabriel croons a string of exaggerated love promises like "you will smile like the first time." I remember his voice blasting from the speakers of our old 1978 Datsun as my father drove the whole family, including my mother, my three brothers and me, around southern Chihuahua, where the domineering desert of our urban world turned into a tree-lined highway following what seemed to me at the time a wide river and thousands and thousands of acres of farmland. As we drove along, I recall, my parents were discussing the crops, trying to decide if the fields were filled with oats or alfalfa. As always, I paid close attention to my parents' chatter, and I remember noticing that on that day in particular their debate—my father had stopped the car to try to prove that he was right—contrasted from its usual tone, lacking any of the rancor with which my parents typically talked to each other. That day was different: my father stopped the car, and I saw both of them walk into the field and then, a few moments later, reemerge from the crop line with the verdict in hand, a verdict that I don't recall and that was never important anyway because what was important to me was that my parents reemerged together, both of them smiling. To me it was a discovery. The crop fields on either side of the highway turned into the feeling, the memory, of a family united. I can hear Juan Gabriel, his voice and the innocuous promises of his song—"this spring the May flowers will be for you"—and that image of my parents stepping together out of the crop fields.

Born in Michoacán, Juan Gabriel was raised and began his career in Juárez, and his musical references to the city—"I like being on the border!" "Juárez is number one!" "The most wonderful border in the world"—are some of the most positive descriptions you can find, especially since the city has become globally known for the extreme violence that descended on it from 2008 to 2012. Juan Gabriel is, indeed, one of the biggest points of pride for a city whose name has become deeply linked with the idea of barbarism.

But Juan Gabriel is not just a promoter of Juárez. He's also an unapologetic spokesman for the Institutional Revolutionary Party (PRI). In 2000, he put on a show in Mexico City's central square as part of the failed campaign of presidential candidate Francisco Labastida, pleading for Mexicans to vote for the party that had been in power for the last seventy-one years.

In 2005, when agents of Felipe Calderón's PAN government arrested Juan Gabriel in the Juárez airport for charges of tax evasion, it was then-mayor and member of the PRI party Héctor "Teto" Murguía who rescued him from Cereso prison, paying his bail so that the "Divo of Juárez" could make his concert at the convocation center which bore his name: the Poliforo Juan Gabriel. He was late to his show but made it nonetheless. He sang for nearly six hours, from after midnight until almost six in the morning. Juan Gabriel's brief visit to the Cereso prison—where he snapped a few photos with some of the inmates—took place in June of 2005, five months before Vicente would first be interned there.

Years later, in May of 2012, the star accompanied Teto in a "surprise" appearance to inaugurate the Monumento a la

Mexicanidad (Monument to Mexicanness), an enormous X-shaped sculpture situated on the border—the project was highly criticized for costing more than 100 million pesos (over $7 million). Teto—a prime example of how the Mexican political machine not only doesn't punish its worst politicians but rather actually rewards them—was reelected in July of 2010, in the midst of the most violent year in the history of the city. By 2012, Teto was riding out the sunset of his second term as murders resulting from the city's drug wars—at least publicly committed murders—had significantly declined to about two murders a day. And yet, even after his reelection—with just a 35 percent voter turnout—he was greeted at the concert by boos. The jeering only ceased when Teto announced Juan Gabriel's presence, who was not there to sing but merely present as Governor César Duarte's guest of honor. The governor, for his part, jumped at the opportunity to announce that the violence was in the past and that the monument's inauguration "should mark the new age of Juárez." Juan Gabriel—no surprise—won over the crowd by improvising a few a cappella lines, which, as always, honored the city. Those familiar with his music certainly recognized the song he was playing on: "I forgot again / that alone under the Juárez moon I loved you." He then dove into his own political message, subscribing to the version that Juárez, after suffering 10,000 murders, had returned to peace. "Here's to a healthy Juárez, because you are healthy, because never again are we going to feel that pain, that anguish, that sadness, that loneliness," said the Divo of Juárez. Looking at it from the right angle, the X of the Monument to Mexicanness behind him resembles, I've always thought, a figure with his hands in the air, as if signaling to someone, "Don't shoot!"

Months later, the adored pop star staged another celebration of the "official end" of the city's narco war, this time for the inauguration of the new Juárez Vive (Juárez Lives) baseball stadium. "Juárez is back, full of enthusiasm for the new days we're living in," Duarte said.

"Never again will they interrupt our lives," Juan Gabriel chimed in.

In front of the Juárez Vive stadium, where 50,000 people danced and sang to the rhythm of the Divo celebrating the city's "recovery," is a two-story building flanked by a yellow fence and metallic palm trees. This building once served as a dance hall. A commercial used to drum up the hall as a place for "stylish and elegant" weddings and *quinceañeras*, promising the safety of security guards and, as a gaudy added bonus, "a spin in a luxury vehicle of your choice: Jaguar, Mercedes Benz, or Hummer."

The business—now closed—was owned by an ex–police officer, whose initials are S.G.E. (I won't name S.G.E. here, as he's still a free man. In 2012, when we first published his, and others', names, I sincerely expected that he would be apprehended and charges would be brought against him and his group—a DEA agent I spoke with in Juárez told me as much. Three years later, however, as it is clear that the Mexican government has taken no steps to apprehend S.G.E., I can only assume that they are protecting him, which makes me hesitate to republish his name.) S.G.E. had served as the chief warrant officer of the attorney general of Northern Chihuahua under Governor Patricio Martínez. He resigned in February of 2004, just days after the federal government arrested thirteen Juárez police officers accused of working with the Juárez Cartel to commit kidnappings, murders and mass burials on the property of a house in the neighborhood of Las Acequias.

S.G.E., who as a sort of side-job to his policing was known to traffic drugs, left his position at the attorney general's office, along with three of his subordinates, without ever facing charges. The four stood apart from the thirteen officers who were arrested and didn't work for the Juárez Cartel but were allegedly part of a distribution team that ferried drugs from Sinaloa to Juárez under the orders of Ismael "El Mayo" Zambada. S.G.E. supervised Zambada's warehouses and any shipments routed to the United States. I became aware of the dance hall in the Melchor Ocampo neighborhood thanks to my colleague Armando, who showed me a picture of the place back in 2007 and told me that S.G.E. was the owner. I later confirmed this in the public records. "Notice the name [of the dance hall]," Armando said, sitting at his desk and pointing to the computer screen. I was looking over his shoulder. The name of the hall was a mash-up of S.G.E.'s and his wife's names.

But neither Armando nor I published a word about the dance hall, and very little, even still, has been published in Juárez about S.G.E.'s role in the fight for control of drug-trafficking routes through northern Mexico. It's undeniable that the Sinaloa Cartel is deadly and eager to retaliate against journalists. It's also undeniable that S.G.E. and his three subordinates have enjoyed total impunity over the past ten years since they walked out of their office during the supposed purge of narcos following the Las Acequias scandal. The four men are not even suspects in the murder of Armando. This despite all evidence linking them to a death threat he received in 2008: Armando received the threat immediately after publishing an article about S.G.E.'s drug-trafficking clan in Juárez, and the incoming number from where the threat was made was traced to the location where S.G.E. purportedly was located. The last death threat I remember *El Diario* receiving, in August of 2011, was also assumed to be from S.G.E.'s clan. Those were the days of relative peace—we had seen a drop from ten homicides a day to five—and *El Diario* came out with an editorial arguing that even though federal troops had arrested the man identified as the leader of the Juárez Cartel (José Antonio Acosta, alias "El Diego"), and even if this man was responsible for more than 1,000 murders, as prosecutors alleged (with no proof aside from a videotaped confession), the city still had to deal with the opposing cartel (the Sinaloa Cartel), locally led by S.G.E. Meanwhile, the threats to our editors warned: "Don't mention those names."

This is how S.G.E., the unmentionable man we suspected was connected to Armando's murder, who owned a business across the street from the stadium where thousands applauded Juan Gabriel in celebration of the city's "recovery," became my personal symbol for deception. What could "recovery" possibly mean for a city drowning in 10,000 uninvestigated murders, including the murder of Armando? What could it mean for a city asphyxiated by a still-present international network of organized crime, full of murderers, full of corrupt ex–police officers, known to many reporters and yet utterly ignored?

This discrepancy in the so-called war against narcos—driven and financed in part by the United States—and the Mexican government's tendency to completely overlook the Sinaloa Cartel became clear to me at the beginning of the military deployment in Juárez, in January of 2008, when, while covering *El Diario*'s military beat, I quickly noticed that most inmates were members of Los Aztecas or police officers who had ties to La Línea, both local cliques of the Juárez Cartel. Though it was easy to document—as a simple statistical analysis unmistakably demonstrates this disparity in arrests—it wasn't until 2010 that the newspaper first ran the story ("This Year Federal Police Detain 31 Members of La Línea ... and Only Four Members of El Chapo's Cartel"). A source I spoke with from the DEA confirmed that the strategy was to do away with La Línea and Los Aztecas first because, as he said, they were responsible for the most "high impact" crimes, such as the 2010 car bomb planted in the city center and the murder of three persons tied to the US Consulate.

Los Aztecas were dangerous, obviously, but equally dangerous were their enemies. And yet no authority would talk about the Sinaloa Cartel. It was only in April of 2012, when the US government presented a formal indictment in El Paso against the activities of the Sinaloa Cartel in Juárez, that we at *El Diario* felt we could publish an article detailing the structure of the cartel and name some of its leading members, including S.G.E.

"The Hunt for El Chapo and 10 Ex–Police Officers"
Staff / El Diario / *Thursday, April 26, 2012*
Ciudad Juárez

This past Tuesday, the US Justice Department revealed that ten of twenty-four Sinaloa Cartel members operating in Chihuahua are ex-officers from the Juárez Municipal Police and the State Police Northern Division.

Testimony presented before the US District Court of West Texas named ex-official S.G.E. (and nine others) as participants in crimes of trafficking, kidnapping, and homicide. The first four named in the report had previously worked in the Warrant Unit of the Attorney General's Office, starting in 2004.

Data from the Department of Justice showed that, in order to maintain their power hold, the cartel employed tactics of intimidation and violence against rivals, informants, the public in general, and the media.

"The purpose of the Enterprise included … enriching the members and associates through, among other things, conspiracy to import and distribute illegal controlled substances, money laundering, and conspiracy to commit murder," according to testimony presented to the Texas Federal Court.

Other objectives included: "preserving and protecting the power, territory and profits of the Enterprise through the use of intimidation, violence, threats of violence, kidnapping, torture and murder … keeping rival traffickers, potential informants, witnesses against the Enterprise, law enforcement, the media and the public at large in fear of the Enterprise and in fear of its members and through threats of violence and violence [sic]."

The indictment also includes a description of the cartel, which was organized under two branches: one composed of death squads and the other dedicated to the storage and trafficking of drugs.

Under this structure, El Chapo's top lieutenants were Núñez Meza, who would later form an independent cell in Durango; Torres Marrufo (arrested), who joined the cartel in 2008 after having worked independently in Villa Ahumada; and Gabino Salas Valenciano (murdered), who controlled the trafficking and territory of the "Gente Nueva" cell in the Juárez Valley.

Both Torres Marrufo and Salas Valenciano, the report describes, led death squads that included some members of Los Artistas Asesinos.

The report continues: "Torres Marrufo oversaw numerous assassin squads dedicated to fighting against La Línea and the Barrio Aztecas ... Torres coordinated cocaine and marijuana shipments to the United States for the Sinaloa Cartel through the Juárez corridor ... Torres Marrufo exclusively used the logo of a 'jaguar' on cocaine bundles to designate his ownership.

"Torres Marrufo received drug proceeds on behalf of the cartel and used some of these proceeds to purchase large quantities of firearms that were imported into Mexico from the United States to support the Sinaloa Cartel's battle with the Juárez Cartel. In furtherance of the Cartel's drug-trafficking and money-laundering activities, Torres Marrufo directed and was responsible for numerous acts of violence."

Torres Marrufo is also believed to be responsible for the abduction and murder of a resident of Horizon City, Texas, who in September of 2008 was found dead in Juárez with his dismembered hands on his chest and a sign on his body that read, "warning to those who might attempt to steal from the Cartel."

Yet another abduction and murder attributed to Torres Marrufo was of a man from Columbus, New Mexico, who was abducted from a wedding at the Señor de la Misericordia Church in Juárez, on the corner of Simona Barba and Valentín Fuentes, along with other guests, including the groom.

At the top of this structure was El Mayo, who had someone known as Germán and S.G.E. (as well as three other ex–police officers) working for him as lieutenants.

The indictment states that before the war between the cartels, S.G.E. would pay a tax to the Sinaloa Cartel in order to be allowed to work as a drug trafficker for the Juárez Cartel.

S.G.E. "oversees security forces and warehouses in Juárez where thousands of kilograms of cocaine are unloaded prior to shipment to the United States … S.G.E. exclusively uses the logo of a cartoon called 'Memín Penguin' on cocaine bundles to designate his ownership." (Memín Penguin was a Mexican cartoon from the 1940s that featured a stereotypical black boy.)

El Diaro's archives indicate that the presumed members of this second cell of the Sinaloa Cartel, which included S.G.E., all resigned from the Warrant Office at the same time, in February of 2004, days after the discovery of twelve bodies buried in a mass grave in the yard of a house in Las Acequias neighborhood.

El Chapo, who Forbes described as one of the richest men in the hemisphere, was finally arrested on February 22, 2014. A team of US agents and Mexican marines raided a luxury condo complex in Mazatlán, Sinaloa, and, without firing a single shot, successfully detained the elusive man.*

Like El Chapo, the rest of the Juárez Cartel's armed wing— including Mario Núñez Meza "Mayito," Antonio Torres Marrufo and Gabino Salas Valenciano—have been arrested or, like Salas Valenciano, murdered.

The band led by El Mayo, however, including Germán and S.G.E., in charge of supervising the storage and distribution of drugs along the border, remains intact.

In October of 2014, I asked the state prosecutor of Chihuahua, Jorge González Nicolás, what the state of Chihuahua had done to investigate the names mentioned in the US indictment.

"I don't look into any of this drug trafficking business," he responded. "It's a business that doesn't concern me. What we do is look into what concerns us."

González served as Vicente León's public defender in 2004.

---

* El Chaps escaped prison for the second time in July of 2015.

"What happened between 2008 and 2010?" González asked himself. "Well, something very simple that shows the cartels' capacity to adapt without anybody [the government] bothering them. I don't know what happened there. I don't want to get involved in that. I don't know whether they [the government] lacked the capacity, or the will, or if they were working with [the Sinaloa Cartel]."

González insisted that his job was to arrest and bring to justice those responsible for common crimes (mostly kidnapping and extortion) and reduce "their firepower." He pointed out that 7,000 firearms had been decommissioned in four years. He stressed the importance of changing the political norms as much as possible so that murderers wouldn't think they could just leave bodies lying in the streets.

González continued: "Today they don't do drive-bys or car-to-car shootings. Now they wait for them to step out of their house in some outlying neighborhood, and that's when they pull the trigger. It's less spectacular now because they don't enjoy the same levels of impunity."

But the city's narcos and organized crime members are still out there, he clarified, after I pressed him about the indictment.

"Of course they're here! We'd be naive to think they'd leave Juárez, or Chihuahua, or even the country, just because, 'Hey, let's leave this place, let's try something else, maybe we could become altar boys, or work in a factory and earn 600 pesos a week.' No! For the cartel as it is, [to put an end to it] we'd need to move the US out of the way. If we could move [Mexico] to Malaysia or if we were neighbors with Finland instead of sitting next to the United States, then maybe. But as for now, no. Chihuahua is on the border."

ACKNOWLEDGMENTS

This book is based on reporting done for *El Diario de Juárez*, largely by me and by Armando Rodríguez (1968–2008). It also relies on the notes of Pedro Sánchez, Luz Sosa, Guadalupe Félix, Ramón Chaparro, Alejandro Gutiérrez, Alejandro Quintero, Araly Castañón, Blanca Carmona, Martín Orquiz, Pedro Torres, Rocío Gallegos, Javier Saucedo, Gabriela Minjares, César Cruz, Roberto Ramos, Cecilia Guerrero, David Alvidrez, Juan Cruz, Lorena Figueroa, Alberto Ponce, Mauricio Rodriguez, Gabriel Acevedo, and Alfredo Ruiz, all from *El Diario*. Also, from *El Norte*'s Felix González, Manuel Aguirre, Carlos Huerta, Salvador Castro, Margarita Hernández and Sonia Aguilar, and *Proceso*'s Patricia Dávila, Ricardo Ravelo and Alejandro Gutiérrez. I have also drawn from "A Juárez Story of Traffickers and the Police," (*New York Times*, December 29, 1999) and "New Adversary in US Drug War: Contract Killers for Mexican Cartels (*Washington Post*, April 4, 2010).